Primetime Proverbs

The Book of TV Quotes

by Jack Mingo
and John Javna

Harmony Books / New York

Dedicated to the scriptwriters who've put
all those great words into the
mouths of TV characters

Published by Harmony Books, a division of Crown Publishers, Inc.,
225 Park Avenue South, New York, New York 10003

HARMONY and colophon are trademarks of
Crown Publishers, Inc.

Library of Congress Cataloging-in-Publication Data

Primetime Proverbs : the book of TV quotes / [compiled by] Jack Mingo.
    p. cm.
1. Proverbs, American. 2. Television programs—United States—
Quotations, maxims, etc.   3. United States—Popular culture.
I. Mingo, Jack, 1952-.   II. Title Prime time proverbs.
PN6427. T45P75   1989
081—dc20   89-2221
                                                              CIP

ISBN 0-517-57284-2
10 9 8 7 6 5 4 3 2 1
First Edition

Contents

Introduction...................... 6
Aging............................9
Ambition.......................10
America........................11
Anger 12
Animals........................12
Arts, The......................13
Average Man, The..............15
Babies 15
Baldness.......................17
Bankers........................18
Bankruptcy....................18
Battle of the Sexes, The.........19
Bees 21
Behind Every Man 21
Bigotry........................22
Booze 23
Boys and Girls 24
Brain, The.....................25
Cads...........................25
Cats 26
Chicken Soup 26
Childhood Ambitions...........27
Christmas 27
Class Consciousness.............28
Coffee 29
Come-Ons.....................30
Common Scents................32
Cops 33
Cops: Tough Talk 35
Cosmic Questions 37
Cosmic Truths..................39
Country & Western Music 44
Courage 44
Cowardice 45
Credit 46
Crime 46
Crooks 47
Crying.........................48
Culture 48
Dating.........................49
Death..........................51

Detectives 53
Diets 53
Divorce........................54
Doctors........................55
Dogs...........................56
Dreams 57
Earth...........................59
Eating 60
Elvis...........................62
Embarrassment.................62
Enemies 63
Ethnic Remarks................63
Evil 65
Experience.....................66
Faith 69
Facts of Life, The 67
Family..........................70
Fashion 71
Fat 72
Fathers 73
Fear 74
Food...........................75
Food for Thought...............78
Food: What Goes Down Must
   Come Up...................79
Freedom.......................79
Free Enterprise 80
Freeways 81
Friends 81
Gambling 82
God 83
Golden Years, The 85
Golf 86
Good Looks 86
Good Samaritans 87
Gossip.........................88
Grandparents 88
Greatness......................88
Greed..........................89
Greens 89
Growing Up 90
Guilt...........................91

Guns 91
Halls of Justice, The 93
Health 94
Heaven 94
Heroes 95
Higher Education 96
History 98
Home 99
Home Improvement 100
Homosexual Panic 101
Honesty 101
Horses 102
Identity 103
If Brains Was Lard 103
Immortality 104
Individuality 105
Insurance 105
Kung Phooey 106
Latin 107
Law, The 108
Lawyers 109
Laziness 110
Leaders and Followers 110
Learning 111
Legal Fees (fantasy) 112
Legal Fees (reality) 113
Lies 113
Life 114
Life's a Bitch 115
Life in the Fast Lane 117
Life: Is That All There Is? ... 117
Life: What Is It? 118
Like, Zen 120
Linguistics 125
Lone Wolf, The 126
Los Angeles 127
Love 128
Magic 130
Mail 131
Makeup 132
Mama Said 132
Marriage: Advice to
   Newlyweds 134
Marriage: To Wed or Not to
   Wed? 134

Marriage: Taking the
   Plunge 136
Marriage: The Wedding 137
Marriage: Wedded Bliss 137
Masculinity 142
Material Possessions 143
Men 144
Mental Health 144
Mind, The 146
Mom 147
Money 148
Money Management 150
Morning 151
Music 151
Names 152
Narcissism: The I's Have It .. 153
Nature 154
Nature of Man, The 155
Never Say Never 158
New York City 159
News, The 160
Nice Girls 160
Nonviolence 161
Nostalgia 163
Nuclear War 163
Nudity 164
Opportunity 164
Paranoia 165
Parents 165
Past/Future 167
Peace 168
People 168
Philosophy of Life 169
Playboy Magazine 170
Poetry 171
Politics 172
Postmortem 175
Poverty 176
Power of Money, The 177
Practical Advice 178
Pregnancy 180
Pride 181
Prison 181
Psychiatry 182
Pyramids, The 182

Questions and Answers 183
Raising Kids 183
Reading................................ 184
Relationships 186
Responsibility 188
Revenge 189
Rich, The............................. 190
Romance.............................. 191
Rules of Etiquette 191
Rules to Live By 193
Science 196
Self-Defense........................ 199
Sex....................................... 199
Sex Education...................... 201
Sexual Confusion 202
Shopping 203
Siblings 204
Silence 205
Sin 205
Skewed Sayings 206
Sleep 207
Spiritual Pursuits 207
Sports.................................. 209
Stand Up and Fight
   Like a Man...................... 211
Success and Failure.............. 212
Suicide 213
Superstition 213
Sushi 214
Talent 214
Taxes 215
Teeth 216
Television: Commercials
   According to Hitchcock.. 217
Television: Its Effect............. 218
Television: Its Future........... 219
Television: Programming 219
Television: The Business..... 220
Television: Watching It 222
Temptation.......................... 223
Theft.................................... 223
Thinking.............................. 225
Time 225
Travel 226

Trust....................................227
Truth, The 228
Ugliness...............................230
U.S.A., The 230
Universe, The 231
Violence...............................232
War 233
Weapons 234
Wine 235
Winning...............................235
Woman's Place, A 236
Woman's Work, A 238
Women 240
Women: The Enigma...........242
Wordplay..............................243
Work 245
Work: Promotions.................247
Work: View from the Top ...248
Work: You're Fired................249
The End 250
Acknowledgments.............251
Index................................253
Calling All TV Fans..........256

Introduction

*Proverbs, proverbs, they're so true. Proverbs tell us what
to do. Proverbs help us all to be better Mouseketeers.*

Jimmie Dodd,
The Mickey Mouse Club

As far as we know, this is the first time anyone has put
together a volume of general TV quotes—rather surprising, con-
sidering how popular television is, and how many other collections
of quotes have made it into print.

Maybe people assume there's nothing on television worth
quoting.

Well, there is. . . . But you have to watch a lot of TV to find
it. Hidden somewhere between inane sitcom jokes and "slam-bang"
action is the subtle glue that holds television programs together—bits
of wisdom . . . poignant comments about life . . . even political satire.
It was our mission—once we chose to accept it—to find these nug-
gets.

Now, after a bleary-eyed year of extracting, sorting, categoriz-
ing, and transcribing quotes, we emerge from our total TV immersion
with 1,000+ examples of primetime platitudes, proverbs, parables, and
commentary—secure in the knowledge that the world will be a better,
wiser place for our efforts.

Are we serious?

You may think we've gone bonkers from months of mega-
exposure to the wisdoms of Gracie Allen, Ward Cleaver, Archie Bunker, Gilligan and the Skipper, too, and the Zen guru Maynard G.
Krebs.

And you may be right. Creating this book was an experience
which might have unhinged lesser minds. As many a moth has
learned from candles, exposure to too much brilliance can lead
beyond illumination and into immolation. But fortunately, dozens of
dedicated TV-watchers volunteered to help us, supplying gems from
their favorite programs to supplement our own choices. This is probably all that prevented us from becoming babbling lunatics who lurch
down the street quoting *Mork and Mindy* ("The only thing we have to
fear is sanity itself"), *Riptide* ("Ryder's law: People generally get out of
the way of crazies"), and other sources of TV wisdom.

Although we have risked our sanity to bring you this package
of TV's most interesting comments, don't worry—you are in no
danger. You can safely open this book anywhere and feast on the

wheat of the collected wisdom of the video age, without having to spend thousands of hours among the chaff, as we have done.

And what ages they are, from the Golden Age of Television through the rise of Civilized Westerns (*Wild, Wild West, Gunsmoke*), through the Agrarian Age (*The Andy Griffith Show, The Beverly Hillbillies*), through the Age of Silverman and beyond.

Now . . . is there really wisdom on TV? Or are TV and wisdom a contradiction in terms? We hope not. Because for most Americans, the wisdom they get from TV is about all the wisdom they're going to get.

Think about it. TV has become the source of the mythology and the folklore of our time. Next time you're talking to your pals, casually refer to Icarus or Zeus. Unless they're literature majors, they'll most likely say, "Huh?" But mention the castaways from *Gilligan's Island* or refer to somebody as "a real Eddie Haskell" and you'll find a flash of recognition immediately with almost anybody (even lit majors).

And, of course, people don't read books any more. They figure that any book worth reading will eventually be made into a made-for-TV miniseries anyway, so why bother?

Even in rural communities, you won't find the wizened old codgers hanging around the feed store, waxing eloquent with home-spun wisdom. The new community center is the town video rental store, and the only thing you'll hear from the wizened old codgers is, "Dadburn it, what do you mean you don't have *Attack of the Killer Bimbos?*"

TV, luckily, has stepped forward to fill the homespun-wisdom gap. For most Americans, TV already fulfills one or more of a variety of roles: friend, companion, spouse, lover, newsgiver, gossip, babysitter, hobby, pet, educator, jester, sleep-inducer, even nightlight—so why not advisor and guru as well?

Some educated snobs may scoff at the notion of being able to learn from "the boob tube." Yet when they start leafing through this book, even they may be surprised. TV regularly comments on, or reflects the prevailing attitudes toward, most of the important issues of day-to-day life. There's even a little philosophy thrown in: Has Immanuel Kant said anything more profound than "I reek, therefore I am" (*Cheers*)? Could Walt Whitman improve on the poetry of Ed Norton (of *The Honeymooners*), who once recited: "When the tides of life turn against you, / And the current upsets your boat, / Don't waste those tears on what might have been; / Just lay on your back and float"? And you'd have to read a heck of a lot of Confucius to find anything as good as "You don't need any brains to grow up. It just happens to ya" (Gilbert, *Leave It to Beaver*).

All this wisdom, and entertainment, too. So when you pick up this book, we hope you find the truth, the comfort, and the counsel that all humanity is seeking. Throughout history and across cultures, mystics, and revolutionaries have gone off into the wilderness and desert to receive enlightenment. We have done the same by journeying into the vast wasteland.

Heck, why settle for being mere visionaries when we can be tele-visionaries?

Jack Mingo
John Javna

After the Fact: Our editor asked us to modify a few of these quotes slightly, either to make them gramatically correct, or to make them a little more comprehensible. Should we do it? We were faced with a crisis of conscience. Fortunately, we didn't have to ponder the question long. In one of those strange quirks of fate, a quote arrived in the mail that clarified everything. It read:

"What's the use of a good quotation if you can't change it?"

Dr. Who,
Dr. Who

Aging

"You're never too old to
do goofy stuff."
> Ward Cleaver,
> *Leave It to Beaver*

❖

"I console myself by thinking that maturity is good for us."
> Joe Rosetti,
> *Rosetti and Ryan*

❖

Amos: "I guess Sapphire feels that by falling in love again she can
recapture her youth."
Andy: "I don't know, Amos, it's gonna be pretty hard to capture
anything that got away that long ago."
> *Amos 'n' Andy*

❖

"Those little lines around your mouth, those crow's feet around your
eyes, the millimeter your derriere has slipped in the last decade
—they're all just nature's way of telling you that you've got nine holes
left to play, so get out there and have a good time."
> David Addison,
> *Moonlighting*

❖

Dorothy: "Oh, come on, Blanche. Age is just a state of mind."
Blanche: "Tell that to my thighs."
> *The Golden Girls*

❖

Fred Sanford: "I still want to sow some wild oats!"
Lamont Sanford: "At your age, you don't have no wild oats—you got
shredded wheat!"
> *Sanford and Son*

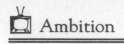
❖

"The real fountain of youth is to have a dirty mind."

Model Jerry Hall,
The Original Max Talking Headroom Show

❖

Judge: "How old are you?"
Grandpa Larkin: "I'm eight-three years young." [In a confidential
tone] "That's what they always say on television so we won't feel
like such old coots."

Mary Hartman, Mary Hartman

Ambition

"I'm tired of being an object of ridicule. I
wanna be a figure of fear, respect, and
SEX!"

Radar O'Reilly,
M*A*S*H

❖

"I want it *all*."

Maude Findlay,
Maude

❖

"There is a passion in the human heart called aspiration. It flares
with a noble flame, and by its light Man has traveled from the caves
of darkness to outer space. But when this passion called aspiration
becomes lust, when its flame is fanned by greed and private hunger,
then aspiration becomes ambition—by which sin the angels fell."

The Control Voice,
The Outer Limits

❖

"My shorts have more ambition than I do."

Alex Reiger,
Taxi

America

[Singing]
"My face may not be handsome, I may be light or fair,
But here in America you're welcome, everybody's welcome
everywhere."

                              The Howdy Doody Show

❖

"There's about three great moments in a man's life: when he buys a
house, and a car, and a new color TV. That's what America is all
about."

                                    Archie Bunker,
                                 All in the Family

❖

"You know what makes this country great? You don't have to be witty
or clever, as long as you can hire someone who is."

                                  Ted Baxter,
                        The Mary Tyler Moore Show

❖

"This is America, where even a horse can dream of living in the
White House."

                                      Mr. Ed,
                                        Mr. Ed

❖

George Jefferson: "It's the American dream come true. Ten years
    ago, I was this little guy with one store. And now look at me—"
Louise Jefferson: "Now you're the little guy with seven stores."

                                    The Jeffersons

❖

"As we move into the hours between darkness and dawn, let's take a
moment to reflect, to say a prayer for all those lost souls destined to
wander this great land of ours, those cheated by life, those who've
been left alone and forsaken, abandoned and ravaged by their dreams.
. . . Goodnight America—wherever you are."

                                  Jack Killian,
                                   Midnight Caller

Anger

"Nothing was ever gained by exchanging words in anger."

Gil Halswell,
Trackdown

❖

"Anger is a lot like a piece of shredded wheat caught under your dentures. If you leave it there, you get a blister and you gotta eat Jell-O all week. If you get rid of it, the sore heals and you feel better."

Sophia,
The Golden Girls

Animals

"Be kind to animals, they'll think you're grand;
Be kind to animals, they'll lick your hand."

Song,
The Howdy Doody Show

❖

"Due to the shape of the North American elk's esaphogus, even if it could speak, it could not pronounce the word *lasagna*."

Cliff Clavin,
Cheers

❖

"Never pet a porcupine."

Anonymous Kid,
Sesame Street

❖

"Dinosaurs are extinct—so you never can tell where they're liable to show up."

Hadji,
Jonny Quest

❖

Gordon Kirkwood [a neighbor]: "You play with this animal like it was human."
Wilbur Post: "There you go with that prejudice again. Are animals

so different from humans? I mean, don't they feel and see and hear and think like humans? Think, Gordon, think. In some other world maybe people will be in cages and animals will be throwing us peanuts."

Kirkwood: "I think you've earned a cage in *this* world."

Mr. Ed

❖

"A professor at Johns Hopkins has come forth with an intriguing thought about a perennial question: He says that if an infinite number of monkeys sat typing at an infinite number of typewriters, the smell in the room would be unbearable."

David Letterman,
Late Night with David Letterman

The Arts

"It is said that art is a human activity, and its purpose is to transmit to others the noblest feelings to which men have risen."

Boris Karloff,
Thriller

❖

Wilbur Post: "Ed, I'm proud of you. Not only do you talk, but you talk beautifully."

Mr. Ed: "Heck, Wilbur, even a chicken would sound good reading Shakespeare."

Wilbur: "Ah, you're a natural, Ed, and with those four legs—why, you could play Romeo and Juliet at the same time."

Mr. Ed

❖

"Actresses are a little weird . . . actresses are artists. Everybody knows that artists have a couple of screws loose."

Chris Cagney,
Cagney & Lacey

❖

"If it weren't for art, there wouldn't be any science."

Penny Robinson,
Lost in Space

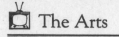
❖

Sponsor [looking at framed picture]: "That's my favorite Picasso. I
have it also."
Rob Petrie: "Oh, do you have one of those prints?"
Mel Cooley: "He has the original."
Rob: "Oh, well, a print has a lot of advantages. If the house blows up,
I'm only out two bucks."

The Dick Van Dyke Show

❖

Det. Ron Harris [an author]: "The contract negotiation. . . . . I tell
you, it's the most important part of the writing process."
Det. Wojohowicz: "I thought it was writin'."
Harris [laughing derisively]: "Yeah, that's what most people think."

Barney Miller

❖

"You know, if Michelangelo had used me as a model, there's no
telling how far he could have gone."

Herman Munster,
The Munsters

❖

"Artists are always ready to sacrifice for art, if the price is right."

Gomez Addams,
The Addams Family

❖

"Irresponsibility isn't a sickness—it's an art."

Remington Steele,
Remington Steele

❖

"Singing opera in the out-of-doors is like painting with oils
underwater—I don't claim the art suffers, but the artist does."

Alfred Hitchcock,
Alfred Hitchcock Presents

The Average Man

"I discovered that the average man—and I guess I'm just about as average as you can get—can't just sit around doing nothing. He's gotta have some incentive to make life interesting and worthwhile."

Howard Sprague,
The Andy Griffith Show

❖

"It is not the physical labor that challenges the average man and woman; it is the constant assaults on the spirit they must learn to endure. The violences against the soul are the ones that hurt the most. The dreams that slip away into middle age; the drudgery of the same job, year after year; the day-to-day compromises; the boss who yells at you—the waiter who looks down his nose because you are wearing the wrong clothes. A thousand tiny attacks that you and I never experience. Because to try to become an average man is to try to become one of the most overlooked, unappreciated, yet noblest creatures of all."

Mr. Roarke,
Fantasy Island

❖

"Everybody gets a crazy desire to be a regular person at some point in their life."

Willie Lawrence,
Family

Babies

"In the short span of nine months, every human embryo passes through a million years of its previous evolution—from protoplasm to fish, to amphibian, to furry ape, to man."

Professor Mathers,
The Outer Limits

❖

Blanche: "I'm reading this Spock book on baby care, and he says it's very important for a young child to have a male role model around during its formative years. Now what are we gonna do? . . ."

Rose: "Oh, Blanche, we don't have anything to worry about. If we give that baby love and attention and understanding, it'll turn out fine."

Dorothy: "That's beautiful."

Rose: "Besides, what does Spock know about raising babies? On Vulcan, all the kids are born in pods."

The Golden Girls

❖

"Home delivery is for newspapers, not babies."

Oscar Madison,
The Odd Couple

❖

"It's an unwritten law: Babies are never born during normal hours."

Danny Williams,
Make Room for Daddy

❖

Sung Hee: "You like the baby?"

Radar O'Reilly: "Yeah, I like all babies—it's a great way to start a life."

M*A*S*H

❖

"Who would have a baby if they thought about what it was going to look like when it was ninety?"

Stephanie Vanderkellen,
Newhart

❖

Pvt. Sam Fender: "Gee, guys, you'd think I committed a crime or something. All my wife did was have a baby."

Pvt. Dino Paparelli: "Your seventh one!"

Pvt. Rocco Barbella: "And every time you have a kid, we have to give you a hundred dollars from the platoon welfare fund."

Sgt. Ernie Bilko: "You like the pitter-patter of little feet. And when one pitter-patter peters out, another pitter-patter patters in."

Fender: "We're thinking of naming this one after you, Ernie."
Bilko: "Forget about me, just call it quits."

The Phil Silvers Show

Baldness

Art Linkletter: "What makes a man bald?"
Kid: "They eat too much. . . . It fills them up so much that it pushes the hair right through the top."

Art Linkletter's House Party

❖

"I cried for the man who had no hair until I met the man with no head."

Bud Lutz,
Eisenhower and Lutz

❖

"Oh, Murray, you're so lucky—other men get dandruff. You get waxy yellow buildup."

Sue Anne Nivens,
The Mary Tyler Moore Show

❖

"Oh, Murray—where did you ever find a party hat made of skin?"

Sue Anne Nivens,
The Mary Tyler Moore Show

❖

"You shouldn't think too much; it makes you bald."

Carlotta,
Bewitched

❖

Buddy Sorrell [to Mel Cooley] : "I wish you'd kept your hair and lost the rest of you."

Sally Rogers: "Watch it Buddy, he'll turn on you."
Buddy: "What's the difference? He's the same on both sides."

The Dick Van Dyke Show

❖

"Never get your hair cut by a bald barber."

Mary Beth Lacey,
Cagney & Lacey

Bankers

Contestant: "You know, bankers never die, they just lose interest."
Groucho Marx: "Not the bankers I know. They'd rather die than lose any interest."

You Bet Your Life

❖

Mr. Drysdale [with money clenched in fist] : "Go ahead, take it."
Jed Clampett: "It would help if you unclenched yore fist."
Jane Hathaway: "What's the trouble?"
Drysdale: "Nothing. Just a muscle spasm. . . . "
Hathaway: "It's happened before. It's an affliction peculiar to bankers. I believe the medical term is lootus-contractus."

The Beverly Hillbillies

❖

"Why do they call them tellers? They never tell you anything. They just ask questions. And why do they call it interest? It's boring. And another thing—how come the Trust Department has all their pens chained to the table?"

Coach Ernie Pantusso,
Cheers

Bankruptcy

"Bankruptcy is so scary it can make you want to suck you own blood."

Count Floyd,
SCTV

The Battle of the Sexes

"You can make a man eat shredded cardboard. . . . If you know the right tricks."

Jeannie's sister,
I Dream of Jeannie

❖

Detective: "Men have always done crazy things around women. Always have, always will."
Tattinger: "Brilliant, detective. Who said that? Hammett? Raymond Chandler?"
Detective: "No, Popeye."

Tattinger's

❖

"Rob, every man makes a fool of himself over a woman sooner or later, and I think the sooner the better."

Steve Douglas,
My Three Sons

❖

Sam Malone: "You've made my life a living hell."
Diane Chambers: "I didn't want you to think I was easy."

Cheers

❖

[To his daughter] "Don't trust guys who wear scarves. And don't trust guys who go too far down with the buttons on their shirt. And don't trust guys who wear too much religious stuff around their neck. . . . I mean, don't trust guys."

Alex Reiger,
Taxi

❖

"Watch out for his biceps—and other protruding parts."

Dee [advising Nancy Dawn about Dakota],
Ryan's Hope

❖

Walter Findlay: "Boy, what a great world this would be without women."

Maude Findlay: "It'd be worth it just to watch you having labor pains."

Maude

❖

Blanche Morton: "Oh, I wish I was a man! I'd knock some of that pompousness out of you."

Harry Morton: "Yes, it's too bad you're not a man. We might have been good friends."

The George Burns and Gracie Allen Show

❖

Blanche Fedders: "Leroy's a terrible patient."

Mary Hartman: "Most men are. I think it's because they're not women. I mean, women have built-in pain. They get cramps once a month, and labor when they have a baby, and men, what do men get? They get a little burning sensation. You know, heartburn. Of course, they do have the army."

Mary Hartman, Mary Hartman

❖

"If she doesn't come to me of her own free will, then I say bring her in on a rope."

Mr. Ed,
Mr. Ed

❖

Cosmetic Clerk: "You know what the fastest way to a man's heart is?"

Roseanne: "Yeah. Through his chest!"

Roseanne

❖

Laura Petrie: "If only Rob weren't so naive when it comes to women. Boy, some of the things he doesn't know. . . . He can be such a little boy, you know?"

Millie Helper: "Then you've got nothing to worry about. It's when he starts acting like a grown man that you have to watch out."

The Dick Van Dyke Show

❖

Ricky Ricardo: "You should be happy you're a woman."
Lucy Ricardo: "Oh, I am, I am!"
Ricky: "You think you know how tough my job is, but believe me, if you traded places with me, you'd be surprised."
Lucy: "Believe me, if I traded places with you, *you'd* be surprised."

I Love Lucy

❖

"Just because we're married to men doesn't mean we've got anything in common with them."

Ethel Mertz,
I Love Lucy

Bees

"Did you know the male bee is nothing but the slave of the queen? And once the male bee has, how should I say, serviced the queen, the male dies. All in all, not a bad system."

Phyllis Lindstrom,
The Mary Tyler Moore Show

❖

"You get more action from a mad bumblebee than you do from a contented one."

Murray Bozinsky,
Riptide

Behind Every Man

Thalia Menninger: "Look at the big picture: What's the future of a boy like Dobie? . . . On his own, I mean."
Herbert T. Gillis: "Black."

Thalia: "Exactly. But, if he had a girl like me, with expensive tastes, why then, he'd have to make a success, wouldn't he?"
Herbert: "Well . . . ."
Thalia: "You show me a financial tycoon and I'll show you, right behind him, a girl like me. We are the movers and the shakers. Why, we take men and we open up their vistas. We broaden their horizons. We just do everything. We make things happen. Dobie is the clay and I am the sculptor."

The Many Loves of Dobie Gillis

❖

Kathy Williams: "Show me a successful man and I'll show you a woman behind him."
Danny Williams: "That's just where she belongs."

Make Room for Daddy

❖

Thurston Howell III: "Gilligan, my boy, let me tell you something. Look behind every successful man, and you will find a woman."
Gilligan: "Yes, sir."
Thurston: "Just make sure his wife doesn't find her."

Gilligan's Island

❖

"A good man doesn't just happen. They have to be created by us women. A guy is a lump like a doughnut. So, first you gotta get rid of all the stuff his mom did to him. And then you gotta get rid of all that macho crap that they pick up from the beer commercials. And then there's my personal favorite, the male ego."

Roseanne,
Roseanne

Bigotry

"For the record, prejudices can kill and suspicion can destroy, and a thoughtless, frightened search for a scapegoat has a fallout of its own—for the children, and the children yet unborn. And the pity of it is that these things cannot be confined to the Twilight Zone."

Rod Serling,
The Twilight Zone

❖

"Look, Archie Bunker ain't no bigot. I'm the first to say—look, it ain't your fault you're colored."

Archie Bunker,
All in the Family

❖

"Bigotry started a long time ago—nobody knows where. Personally I think the French started it."

Johnny Fever,
WKRP in Cincinnati

❖

"Converts are the worst kind of bigots."

Edison Carter,
Max Headroom

❖

"You keep harping about minorities. Well, mister, you're a psycho, and they're minorities, too."

Sgt. Joe Friday,
Dragnet

Booze

Sgt. Joe Friday [to drunk woman] : "Don't you think you've had enough of that?"
Woman: "*Is* there enough?"

Dragnet

❖

"I make it a point never to consume anything that's been aged in a radiator."

Maj. Charles Emerson Winchester III
M*A*S*H

"There is something very suspicious about a man who keeps his booze under lock and key."

Vila Restal,
Blake's 7

❖

"Oh, I just adore beer. It's so . . . so . . . democratic."

Kookie's Girlfriend,
77 Sunset Strip

❖

"Never cry over spilt milk. It could've been whiskey."

Pappy Maverick,
Maverick

Boys and Girls

"Go see a girl? I'd rather smell a skunk!"

Beaver Cleaver,
Leave It to Beaver

❖

"When fishing for boys, the proper bait is girls."

Mary Anne,
Gilligan's Island

❖

"Whoever thought up boys must've made a million dollars."

Patty Lane,
The Patty Duke Show

❖

Dr. Von Pablum (Sid Caesar): "In the makeup of girls the subconscious is always in conflict with the conscious and the ego cannot regard any of the involuntary reflexes which are happening in the present state, the past state, and the future state that cannot be comprehended. And that's the makeup of little girls."

Interviewer (Carl Reiner): "And what are little boys made of?"

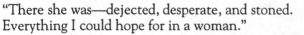
Von Pablum: "Snakes and snails and puppy dog tails. That's what
little boys are made of."

Your Show of Shows

❖

"Any boy who likes cobras, toads, and apes can't be all bad."

Gomez Addams,
The Addams Family

The Brain

"My theory about the brain is that the brain is bigger than the mind.
The brain is everything. The whole shooting match. But the mind is
nothing. You want to cross your legs you need the brain. The mind
can't make up its mind. And the heart is just a pump and the liver is
just for laughs. The brain is everything."

Professor Ludwig von Brenner (Sid Caesar),
Your Show of Shows

❖

"If ever we needed a brain, now is the time."

Squiggy Squiggman,
Laverne and Shirley

Cads

"It's terrible what's happening on the streets today. Last week I got
badly beaten up fighting for a woman's honor. Next
time I'll pick a smaller woman."

Henry Gibson,
Laugh-In

❖

"There she was—dejected, desperate, and stoned.
Everything I could hope for in a woman."

Louie DePalma,
Taxi

Cats

"The thing about cats is that they will always love you, as long as it's your hand that holds the can opener."

> Loretta,
> *Another World*

❖

"The only good cat is a stir-fried cat."

> Alf,
> **ALF**

❖

"Once a bad ol' puddy tat, always a bad ol' puddy tat!"

> Tweety Bird,
> *The Bugs Bunny Show*

Chicken Soup

Mary Hartman: "Chicken soup is very good for you. Chicken soup is good for anything that ails you. It may not be good for, like, if you're bleeding internally or broken bones, but it's good for anything else that ails you. Now do you understand that?"
Coach Leroy Fedders: "Who says that, Mary?"
Mary: "An entire ethnic group, Leroy. The whole Jewish people. And they ought to know. I mean, they practically invented chicken soup. And an incredible amount of those people are doctors."

> *Mary Hartman, Mary Hartman*

❖

Janet: "I thought chicken soup was the universal cure-all."
Cecilia: "Not for fleshwounds."

> *Simon and Simon*

Childhood Ambitions

Floyd Lawson: "I always did want to be a barber, even when I was a little kid. I used to practice on cats. I'd catch them in the alley and then I'd clip them. We had the baldest cats in the county."
Andy Taylor: "That's a fact, and folks still say that Floyd ain't much with people, but he's a great cat barber."
The Andy Griffith Show

❖

The Skipper: "I always thought I'd like to be a cowboy."
Thurston Howell III: "Somewhere there breathes a horse who's glad you are not."
Gilligan's Island

❖

Dr. Compton: "What would you like to do in life?"
Beaver Cleaver: "Well, I think maybe a garbage collector."
Dr. Compton: "Now, why a garbage collector?"
Beaver: "Well, you don't have to wash your hands all the time and nobody cares how you smell."
Leave It to Beaver

❖

"I don't like to brag, but I'm really a pretty unusual guy. I mean, you take lots of guys in their twenties, or even in their thirties. They're still floundering around looking for their life's work. Not me. I've known for years what my life's work is—girls."
Dobie Gillis,
The Many Loves of Dobie Gillis

Christmas

"It's Christmas! Time for miracles on Thirty-fourth Street, angels with wings, a fat man being pulled around by a dozen antelope."
Starman,
Starman

❖

Kid: "I saw Santa Claus come right over to my bed and hang up a stocking full of presents."
Art Linkletter: "What did he look like?"
Kid: "Well, he was wearing pajama tops, and carrying a bottle of beer."

Art Linkletter's House Party

❖

"There's a wondrous magic to Christmas, and there's a special power reserved for little people. In short, there's nothing mightier than the meek, and a merry Christmas to each and all."

Rod Serling,
The Twilight Zone

❖

"Dear Santa, I'd like to be taller, but if not, please reconsider my application for elf."

Arnold Horschack,
Welcome Back, Kotter

Class Consciousness

"The name of my new girl is Samantha Digby. Samantha comes from very high society. She has wealth, breeding, social position, blue blood. Whereas I am the son of a plain, simple grocer, Herbert T. Gillis. But does Samantha care that she's from the upper crust and I'm from the hoi polloi? Of course she doesn't. And why doesn't she? Because she doesn't know. And why doesn't she know? Because I lied to her."

Dobie Gillis,
The Many Loves of Dobie Gillis

❖

"Let's face it. I'm just not the type to have a maid. Some people are cut out for champagne and caviar; I'm the beer and pretzel type."

Lucy Ricardo,
I Love Lucy

❖

Sapphire: "I've never been to a home like Mrs. Van Pelt's—she's real society!"
Kingfish: "Oh, so you're mixin' up with the hoi polluted?"

Amos 'n' Andy

❖

"If God had not meant for there to be poor people, He wouldn't have given you all their money."

Revivalist minister addressing a wealthy congregation,
SCTV

❖

"As my old Pappy used to say, if the Lord had more respect for money he'd have given it to a better class of people."

Bret Maverick,
Bret Maverick

❖

Jed Clampett: "We'll commence plowing tomorrow."
Banker [horrified]: "This is *Beverly Hills*."
Jed: "Dirt is dirt."

The Beverly Hillbillies

Coffee

Sister Mary Catherine: "Do you make good coffee?"
Hoss Cartwright: "Ma'am, that's one thing a bachelor learns to do well."

Bonanza

❖

"Most people just don't know how to make good coffee. In the first place, they boil the water before they put the coffee in. Any fool knows you gotta put the coffee in the cold water and bring 'em both to the boil together. That way you get all the flavor. Worst thing they do, they throw away the old grounds after using them once. What they don't know is they're throwing away the best part. You gotta keep them old grounds an' you add a little fresh coffee every mornin' and let 'er boil. Shoot, you don't make a cup, you build a pot. You don't really get a good pot until you've been usin' it about a week. Then it's coffee."

Chester Goode,
Gunsmoke

❖

"Make my coffee like I like my men: hot, black, and strong."

Willona Woods,
Good Times

❖

"*Wine* is for aging, not coffee."

Ken Hutchinson,
Starsky and Hutch

❖

Barney Miller: "Any coffee left?"
Nick Yemana: "You must be a glutton for punishment."

Barney Miller

Come-ons

Laura Holt: "A magnum of champagne?"
Remington Steele: "You looked thirsty."
Laura: "Do you always do things on such a grand scale?"
Remington: "Only when I'm aroused . . . with curiosity."

Remington Steele

❖

Movie Starlet: "Would you care for a drink?"
Jeff Spencer: "It's a little early."
Movie Starlet: "Time is relative, Mr. Spencer. When I first saw you, I
immediately thought of a martini."

77 Sunset Strip

❖

"If they had you in my size, I'd take you in every color."

Joey Germaine,
McMillan and Wife

❖

"Have I got an evening planned for us! I already called room service,
and they're sending up champagne, canapes . . . and oxygen!"

Louie DePalma,
Taxi

❖

Flo Castleberry [waiting on a customer]: "Hi, handsome. What'll it
be?"
Customer: "Well, what have you got in mind?"
Flo: "If it's the same thing you have in mind, you ain't gonna find it
on the menu."

Alice

❖

"Y'know, Henry, without getting gushy, you're the man I'd love to get
stranded on Gilligan's Island with."

Amy Cassidy,
Bosom Buddies

❖

"You American girls have such big breasts all the time. . . . So, please
give us the number of your apartment so we can go up there and have
sex with you now!"

Dan Aykroyd (the Wild and Crazy Guy),
Saturday Night Live

❖

[In the fruit section of a supermarket]

Nick Ryder: "Hi. Look, I—you gotta excuse me. I know this is gonna sound kind of weird, okay? But I don't know how to pick a ripe cantaloupe, and I was just watching you shake that cantaloupe, but I was wondering, what are you supposed to hear when you shake that? Is there a little voice in there that says 'pick me' . . . or what?"

Lt. Joanna Parisi: "Well, if you hear the seeds squishing around a lot, it usually means the melons are pretty ripe."

Nick: "Uh-huh. So if I were to shake that cantaloupe, I would hear the seeds shaking around in there, right?"

Joanna: "Uh-huh."

Nick: "Can I shake your cantaloupe?"

Joanna: "Be my guest."

Riptide

❖

Jennifer Hart [rubbing a Buddha-type figure]: "It's supposed to bring you luck."

Jonathan Hart: "If you rub my stomach like that, I'll bring you anything you want."

Hart to Hart

Common Scents

Gracie Allen: "Something smells good."

Peter: "It's Mr. Morton's ribs."

Gracie: "Really? George only puts cologne on his *face*."

The George Burns and Gracie Allen Show

❖

Mark Royer: "Smells good."

Barbara Cooper: "It's Rock Cornish game hen."

Mark: "Smells more like Chanel."

Barbara: "Oh!"

Mark: "My favorite."

Barbara: "Chanel?"

Mark: "Game hen."

Barbara: "Well, next time I'll just put a little chicken grease behind each ear."

One Day at a Time

❖

Grandpa: "UMMMM. What smells so good?"

Herman Munster: "I cut myself shaving."

The Munsters

❖

Marian Cunningham: "Doesn't Richie look nice tonight?"

Joanie Cunningham: "He has stinky stuff on his hair."

Howard Cunningham: "Oh, is that what the smell is? I thought the milk had gone sour."

Happy Days

Cops

"If you really want to study police methods, do what I do: watch television."

Officer Gunther Toody,
Car 54, Where Are You?

❖

[To a young man who wants to be a cop] "Listen to me, son . . . let me give you the hard facts. When you put on that uniform you're a marked man—marked by the supercritical eyes of the public, marked by the guns of every hoodlum you chase into a corner. You work around the clock, half your life in darkness, and you sleep the other half . . . away from God's good sunshine. You're strictly a second-class citizen. You can't enter controversial subjects in public, you can't enter a political campaign, you can't even write a letter to the editor. You make one mistake, you're a headline."

> **Dan Muldoon,**
> *Naked City*

❖

"When you're a lawman and you're dealing with people, you do a whole lot better if you go not so much by the book but by the heart."

> **Andy Taylor,**
> *The Andy Griffith Show*

❖

"No man who has never worn a badge has the right to judge the courage of one who has."

> **Luke Rumbaugh,**
> *Gunsmoke*

❖

Det. Arthur Dietrich: "Maybe it's true. Maybe I do have different values. Maybe I just happen to have a stronger philosophical foundation than the rest of you. Is that my fault?"
Det. Ron Harris: "Then why'd you become a cop in the first place?"
Dietrich: "I stood in the wrong line."

> *Barney Miller*

❖

Art Linkletter: "What do you want to be?"
Kid: "A policeman."
Art: "What's the most important thing to remember to be a good policeman?"
Kid: "Don't wet your bed."

> *Art Linkletter's House Party*

Cops: Tough Talk

Crook [explaining herself]: "You can understand, can't you?"
Sgt. Joe Friday: "No, lady, we can't. You're under arrest."

Dragnet

Witness [refusing to testify, because he doesn't want to "get involved"]: "Mr. Friday, if you was me, would you want to testify?"
Sgt. Joe Friday: "Can I wait awhile?"
Witness: "Huh?"
Friday: "Before I'm you."

Dragnet

❖

Mother of Juvenile Delinquent [about her son]: "People just don't understand the boy."
Sgt. Joe Friday: "San Quentin is full of people who are hard to understand."

Dragnet

❖

Killer: "You made a mistake, and I'm not going to pay for it."
Sgt. Joe Friday: "You going to use a credit card?"

Dragnet

❖

Crook: "Well, Templar, let's have it. What do you want?"
Simon Templar (The Saint): "I just wanted to see how the other half lives—the rotten half."

The Saint

❖

Guilty Woman: "Listen to me—"
Peter Gunn: "A jury's going to listen to you. You're going to get about ten years."

Peter Gunn

❖

"Another outburst like this and I'm gonna handcuff your lips together."

Sgt. Wojohowicz,
Barney Miller

❖

[To Dudley Do-Right]
"Do-Right, you're a disgrace to your underwear."

Inspector Fenwick,
The Bullwinkle Show

❖

[To a hood getting up from a table] "If you're not growin', sit down."

Sgt. Joe Friday,
Dragnet

❖

"Your tragedy is our incentive; we just love to see nice people get in trouble."

Arthur Dietrich,
Barney Miller

❖

"Would you like to sit down, hairball, or do you prefer internal bleeding?"

Mick Belker,
Hill Street Blues

Reluctant Informer: "I got nothin' to say, Ness."
Eliot Ness: "Hmmm . . . the code of bums—lips sealed tight. You stick to that code and your lips will be sealed tight forever."

The Untouchables

❖

Dying Hood: "I [gasp, cough] I didn't do bad, did I?"
Eliot Ness [stone-faced, philosophical]: "No, you didn't do bad. You just got yourself killed."

The Untouchables

Cosmic Questions

"Why do they call it rush hour when nothing moves?"

Mork,
Mork and Mindy

❖

"Should rapists be castrated at birth?"

Twiggy Rathbone,
Hot Metal

❖

"It makes you wonder, doesn't it? Just how normal are we? Just who are the people we nod our hellos to as we pass on the street? A rather good question to ask—particularly in the Twilight Zone."

> Rod Serling,
> *The Twilight Zone*

❖

"Is love like a pain that doesn't hurt?"

> Biddie Cloom,
> *Here Come the Brides*

❖

"Have you ever thought how nice it would be to have a woman of your own to saw in half?"

> Lucy Ricardo,
> *I Love Lucy*

❖

"Does a turkey laugh at an axe?"

> Samantha Stevens,
> *Bewitched*

❖

"How can we maintain the highest standard of living in the world when our ice cream tastes like garage doors?"

> Bat-Bat,
> *The New Adventures of Mighty Mouse*

❖

"I wonder what purpose junk mail has in the grand scheme of things?"

> Chris Cagney,
> *Cagney & Lacey*

❖

"There is a theory that Earth and sun and galaxy and all the known universes are only a dust-mote on some policeman's uniform in some gigantic superworld. Couldn't we be under some supermicroscope, right now?"

> The Control Voice,
> *The Outer Limits*

❖

Emily Hartley: "Bob and I are giving a Fourth of July party—would you like to come?"
Howard Borden: "Oh, great! When is it?"

The Bob Newhart Show

Cosmic Truths

"It is an important and popular fact that things are not always as they seem."

Narrator,
The Hitchhiker's Guide to the Galaxy

❖

"A truly wise man never plays leapfrog with a unicorn."

Banacek,
Banacek

❖

"Remember always—a wise man walks with his head bowed, humble like the dust."

Master Po,
Kung Fu

❖

"You got to know the rules before you can break 'em. Otherwise, it's no fun."

Sonny Crockett,
Miami Vice

❖

"Certain things in our universe are fixed and absolute. The sun always rises in the east. Parking meters are always set to give an edge to the meter maid. And sons never phone."

Brian Devlin,
The Devlin Connection

❖

"That's why they made tomorrow—so we don't have to do everything today."

Betty Jones,
Barnaby Jones

❖

"You can lead a herring to water, but you have to walk really fast or they die."

Rose,
The Golden Girls

❖

"Professionals should not let a man turn himself into a small furry animal right in front of their eyes."

Rick Simon,
Simon and Simon

❖

"One thing is for sure—a sheep is not a creature of the air."

Graham Chapman,
Monty Python's Flying Circus

❖

"Practicality is the last refuge of the mediocre."

Dr. Miguelito Loveless,
The Wild, Wild West

❖

"Some men try to climb mountains. Others just date them."

Louie DePalma,
Taxi

❖

"Most people's lives are governed by telephone numbers."

Narrator,
The Hitchhiker's Guide to the Galaxy

❖

"If you don't show up to a party, everyone will assume you're fat."
Stephanie Vanderkellen,
Newhart

❖

"There's nothing more sophomoric than men contemplating their own hormones."
Chris Cagney,
Cagney & Lacey

❖

"There's a time to be Daniel Boone, and there's a time to be a plumber."
MacGyver,
MacGyver

❖

"Out of every disaster, a little progress is made."
The Control Voice,
The Outer Limits

❖

"A woman does not break into your house and clean it for fun."
Rick Simon,
Simon and Simon

❖

"When your pants go in the hamper, whatever's inside becomes public domain."
Valerie Hogan,
Valerie

❖

"If you don't stand for something, you'll fall for anything."
Michael Evans,
Good Times

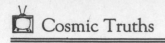
❖

"No good deed ever goes unpunished."

B.J. Hunnicut,
M*A*S*H

❖

"There is nothing you can do with a really dedicated misfit."

Robot,
Lost in Space

❖

"Quantity is never a worthy substitute for quality, whether it is in the choice of a book, a play, a friend, or a gun."

Paladin,
Have Gun, Will Travel

❖

"You never get a second chance to make a first impression."

Head and Shoulders **commercial**

❖

"Nothing is as powerful as a joke whose time has come."

Charlie Moore,
Head of the Class

❖

"If you've wrecked one train,
you've wrecked them all."

Gomez Addams,
The Addams Family

❖

"When the reckless hunter sets a trap, he often becomes its first victim."

> German Officer,
> *Combat*

❖

"There's a big difference between making instant coffee and bringing a Rastafarian back from the dead."

> Ricardo Tubbs,
> *Miami Vice*

❖

"Nothing strengthens the character like a little misfortune."

> Friar Tuck,
> *The Adventures of Robin Hood*

❖

"Man can only doodle on his napkin for so long."

> Remington Steele,
> *Remington Steele*

❖

"Hamster milk picks up where turtle oil fears to tread."

> Mr. Haney,
> *Green Acres*

❖

"Time has little to do with infinity and jelly donuts."

> Thomas Magnum,
> *Magnum, P.I.*

❖

"The only thing harder to get rid of than a winter cold is a 1973 Ford Pinto."

> Aileen Foster,
> *Double Trouble*

Country & Western Music

"You don't understand country and western music. It's about the real things in life—murder, train wrecks, amputations, faucets leakin' in the night—all stuff like that."

Charlie Haggars,
Mary Hartman, Mary Hartman

❖

"There's nothing like a hardship song to set my toes a-tappin'."

Roseanne,
Roseanne

Courage

The Professor: "Discretion is sometimes the better part of valor."
Thurston Howell III: "Discretion is *always* the better part of valor."

Gilligan's Island

❖

"When a man faces trouble, he doesn't have to worry about his back."

Pat Garrett,
The Tall Man

❖

"There's different kinds of bravery. It's a whole lot easier to be brave saving yourself than it is when it means saving someone else."

Hoby Gilman,
Trackdown

❖

"Wanna do something courageous? Come to my house and say to my mother-in-law, 'You're wrong, fatso!' "

Buddy Sorrell,
The Dick Van Dyke Show

❖

"A man never knows how tall a shadow he'll cast 'til he stands up."

Hoby Gilman,
Trackdown

❖

"If you're gonna throw in the towel, sit on a sword, not a goddurn tamale."

Howard Hunter,
Hill Street Blues

Cowardice

Lionel "Brown Shoe" Whitney: "Why don't you just admit you're chicken and be done with it?"
E.L. "Tenspeed" Turner: "All right, I'm chicken. But I'm a pragmatic chicken. And those are the best kind, because they never end up swimming around with the potatoes and gravy."

Tenspeed and Brown Shoe

❖

"He who chickens out and runs away will chicken out another day."

Robot,
Lost in Space

❖

"My Pappy always said, 'A coward dies a thousand deaths, a hero dies but one.' A thousand to one is pretty good odds."

Bret Maverick,
Maverick

❖

"A coward dies a hundred deaths, a brave man only once. . . . But then, once is enough, isn't it?"

Judge Harry Stone,
Night Court

Credit

Walter Denton: "Oh that's a neat coat. When did you buy it?"
Connie Brooks: "Within the next eighteen months."

Our Miss Brooks

Crime

"Throughout history, compassionate minds have pondered this dark and disturbing question: What is society to do with those members who are a threat to society, those malcontents and misfits whose behavior undermines and destroys the foundations of civilization?"

The Control Voice,
The Outer Limits

❖

"Murder can be exhausting."

Amos Burke,
Burke's Law

❖

"If society is at fault that we got killers running around murdering innocent people, then it's simple: We turn the killer loose, give him a pension for life, and shoot the rest of the city."

Archie Bunker,
All in the Family

❖

"Is it really a crime to rid the world of car dealers?"

The Widow Cody,
The Widow Cody

❖

"If a city wants to keep law and order, it's got to kick people around."

Wally Cleaver,
Leave It to Beaver

❖

"All persons attempting to conceal criminal acts involving their cars are hereby warned: Check first to see that underneath that chrome there does not lie a conscience, especially if you're driving along a rain-soaked highway in the Twilight Zone."

Rod Serling,
The Twilight Zone

❖

"It's a proven fact that capital punishment is a known detergent for crime."

Archie Bunker,
All in the Family

❖

"Al Capone is dead. Eliot Ness is dead. But the struggle between the Capones and Nesses, witnessed by a public that is dangerously indifferent, goes on and on.

Walter Winchell (narrator),
The Untouchables

Crooks

Friend of a Suspect: "I just know she isn't guilty. She's just too nice."
Sgt. Joe Friday: "Well, if she's nice, she isn't guilty."
Friend: "Yes."
Friday: "And if she's guilty, she's not that nice."

Dragnet

❖

Crook: "I don't know what's wrong with me. The other guys I know who are making it big in crime, they're vicious, they're ruthless, they'd shoot you just as soon as look at you. But not me. Last week I went to hold up a liquor store in Queens. Who's running it? Vietnamese refugees. I wound up giving 'em twenty bucks to help

the boat people. I don't know what my problem is."
Wojo Wojohowicz: "Maybe you're just a decent human being."
Crook [offended]: "Hey, I feel bad enough already."

Barney Miller

❖

Rush: "Lincoln wasn't a crook."
Wainwright: "We don't know that. He never finished his term."

Too Close for Comfort

Crying

Rob Petrie: "Oh, honey, please, I hate to see you cry like this."
Laura Petrie: "Well, it's the only way I know how to cry."

The Dick Van Dyke Show

Culture

"Culture is like spinach. Once you forget it's good for you, you can relax and enjoy it."

Uncle Martin,
My Favorite Martian

❖

"For civilization to survive, the human race has to remain civilized."

Rod Serling,
The Twilight Zone

❖

"I wish I knew how customs like this get started; it would make them easier to stamp out."

Martin Lane,
The Patty Duke Show

"Being a [product] of the consumer culture, I sometimes forget to be a human being."

Illya Kuryakin,
The Man from U.N.C.L.E

❖

"You can't let a job stifle your mind, buddy boy. You've got to keep yourself free for cultural pursuits, you know. . . . Good reading, good music . . . bowling."

Mike Stone,
The Streets of San Francisco

Dating

"Early to bed, early to rise, and your girl goes out with other guys."

Bob Collins,
Love That Bob

❖

"Carmine and I have an understanding. I'm allowed to date other men, and he's allowed to date ugly women."

Shirley Feeney,
Laverne and Shirley

❖

Dorothy: "How was your date with Blanche?"
Ted: "Oh, I don't know. . . . Maybe I'm old-fashioned, but when I was

dating, the man used to make all the moves."
Dorothy: "How many men have you dated?"

The Golden Girls

❖

Pvt. Doberman: "Sarge, I don't know what to do around girls. I'm scared."
Sgt. Bilko: "It's not your fault. It's the army's fault. They keep giving us the wrong basic training."

The Phil Silvers Show

❖

Felix Unger [reminiscing about his first date]: "When I took her home, I didn't try to kiss her or anything like that. I was a perfect gentleman. I've never forgotten it."
Oscar Madison: "I'll bet *she* did."

The Odd Couple

❖

"Ramon is no gentleman; that's why I'm so anxious to go out with him."

Esmeralda,
Bewitched

❖

Janet Wood: "When you take a girl out and you go to get her, don't you like it if she's dressed and ready?"
Jack Tripper: "No. . . . Just ready."

Three's Company

❖

"In my town, we didn't have datin'. You washed your hair every Saturday night and when you were fourteen, you married your cousin."

Nurse Laverne,
Empty Nest

❖

"Randy, there are three reasons why I won't go out with you: one, you're obnoxious; two, you're repulsive; and three, you haven't asked me yet."

Julianne,
Van Dyke

Death

"Death is just nature's way of telling you, 'Hey, you're not alive anymore.'"

Bull,
Night Court

❖

"It is inevitable. A man must die a little every day."

Illya Kuryakin,
The Man from U.N.C.L.E.

❖

"Like women all over America, my mother confronted tragedy and death with cold ham and Jell-O salad."

Kevin Arnold,
The Wonder Years

❖

"Cigarettes can kill, but so can love, and so can Lola."

Lola Heatherton,
SCTV

❖

"There shouldn't be heart attacks . . . or cancer, or anything like that. There should just be a certain age where ya have to turn your life in—like a library book. You pack a bag. You go—and that's that."

Rose,
The Golden Girls

❖

"I'd rather live in vain than die *any* way."

Bart Maverick,
Maverick

❖

"Abracadabra, the guy's a cadaver."

David Addison,
Moonlighting

❖

"You can't kill me . . . because I am already dead."

Barnabas Collins,
Dark Shadows

❖

"There's a saying: 'Every man is put on Earth condemned to die, time and method of execution unknown.' Perhaps this is as it should be."

Rod Serling,
The Twilight Zone

❖

"Anybody who would die for a practical joke deserves to get his laugh."

Rob Petrie,
The Dick Van Dyke Show

❖

"Well, Norton, I guess there'll be no more bus rides for me. I've come to the end of the line. I'm going to that big bus depot in the sky. It's a one-way trip with no transfers."

Ralph Kramden,
The Honeymooners

Detectives

"I'm engaged in a project that is going to benefit mankind and keep the streets of our country safe for women and children everywhere. I'm a detective."

Herman Munster,
The Munsters

❖

Client: "I think it's really exciting walking up to people saying , 'Have you seen this man?' "
Jim Rockford: "Really exciting. On the excitement scale it rates somewhere between a haircut and root canal work."

The Rockford Files

❖

Della Street: "You're a cynic. You keep looking for things that just aren't there."
Perry Mason: "Of course, when a man looks for things that aren't there and finds them, we call him a detective."

Perry Mason

Diets

Jessica Tate: "Eunice, how would you like some pancakes for breakfast?"
Eunice Tate: "No thank you, Mother. I'm on three hundred calories a day."
Jessica: "Three hundred calories! But darling, what can you eat?"
Eunice: "Nothing. If I brush my teeth twice a day, that puts me a little over."

Soap

❖

Mary Richards: "Want any fruit?"
Rhoda Morgenstern: "Naw, I'm still on my diet—got any wax fruit?"
The Mary Tyler Moore Show

❖

"I seem to have lost some weight and I don't wish to mar my image. I cannot reveal exactly how much weight. I can only say that had I lost ten more pounds, I would have had to file a missing persons report."

Alfred Hitchcock,
Alfred Hitchcock Presents

❖

Norm Peterson: "How do you keep so trim, Carla?"
Carla Tortelli: "Sex."
Norm: "You mean sex is the greatest exercise?"
Carla: "Nah. I miss it so much I can't eat."

Cheers

❖

"Look at how chubby I am. . . . Look at my ears, how fat they are. My eyeballs don't fit in their sockets anymore. And look at this jacket—it used to be a topcoat. . . . Yep, today's the day I'm gonna do it. . . . Today's the day I'm going on a diet. . . . I gotta have will power. . . . I gotta be strong . . . and I gotta have a lot of strength. . . . So make me a big breakfast, 'cause I gotta have a lot of strength to go with this diet!"

Sid Caesar,
Your Show of Shows

Divorce

Groucho Marx: "What are you gonna do with your money, Colonel?"
Man: "I'm gonna make my wife happy, Groucho."
Groucho: "What are you gonna do—get a divorce?"

You Bet Your Life

❖

"Actress Robin Givens has filed a libel suit against estranged husband Mike Tyson, claiming he told a reporter that she was after his money. . . . She's asking $125 million."

NBC News

❖

Barbara Cooper: "I want to remember Dad the way it was when the four of us were together."
Julie Cooper: "Yeah, he's so much happier now."

One Day at a Time

❖

Dinner Guest #1: "Does your wife understand you?"
Dinner Guest #2: "I'm not married. But my previous three wives understood me perfectly . . . which is why each marriage failed so dismally."

The Saint

❖

"Did you ever stop to think that alimony is like keeping up the payments on a car with four flats?"

Laugh-In

Doctors

Cmdr. John Koenig: "Why do doctors make the worst patients?"
Dr. Helena Russell: "Probably because we know too much."

Space: 1999

❖

"All them surgeons—they're highway robbers. Why do you think they wear masks when they work on you?"

Archie Bunker,
All in the Family

❖

"This warning from the New York City Department of Health Fraud: Be suspicious of any doctor who tries to take your temperature with his finger."

David Letterman,
Late Night with David Letterman

❖

"When I had my operation, the doctor gave me a local anesthetic. I couldn't afford the imported kind."

Laugh-In

❖

"Think of the money in hospitals. Do you know the mark-up on oxygen alone? Fantastic. And the poor customers, there's nothing they can do. You've got 'em flat on their backs!"

Thalia Menninger,
The Many Loves of Dobie Gillis

❖

Henry Blake: "I was never very good with my hands."
Radar O'Reilly: "Guess that's why you became a surgeon, huh Sir?"

M*A*S*H

❖

Sophia: "How come so many doctors are Jewish?"
Jewish Doctor: "Because their mothers are."

The Golden Girls

Dogs

"You're glad to see me every minute of my life. I come home, you jump around and wag your tail. I go in the closet, I come out, you jump around and wag your tail. I turn my face away, I turn it back, you wag your tail. Either you love me very much or your short-term memory is shot."

Dr. Harry Weston,
Empty Nest

❖

Imogene Coca: "Dogs are really faithful. We had a neighbor of ours who treated his dog miserably . . . never fed him on time. Well, one day he just up and left. That dog didn't leave that front porch. He was faithful. Well, about two years later, the master returned. The

dog just stood there, watching his master come down the path and onto the porch."
Sid Caesar: "And then what happened?"
Coca: "Ripped him to pieces."

Your Show of Shows

❖

"He who lies down with dogs gets up with fleas."

Herman Munster,
The Munsters

Dreams

"We know that a dream can be real, but who ever thought that reality could be a dream? We exist, of course, but how, in what way? As we believe, as flesh-and-blood human beings, or are we simply part of someone's feverish, complicated nightmare? Think about it, and then ask yourself, do you live here, in this country, in this world, or do you live instead . . . in the Twilight Zone?"

Rod Serling,
The Twilight Zone

❖

"It is said that a man's life can be measured by the dreams he fulfills."

Mr. Roarke,
Fantasy Island

❖

"Dreams are the soul's pantry. Keep it well stocked and your soul will never hunger."

Shirley Feeney,
Laverne and Shirley

❖

"If you stop dreaming, you're just wasting eight hours a night."

David Addison,
Moonlighting

❖

"Dreams are the true interpreters of our desires."

Dr. Smith,
Lost in Space

❖

"Some of us, in dreams, cannot reach beyond the walls of our own little sleep."

The Control Voice,
The Outer Limits

❖

"The only thing I ever dream is that I just won every beauty contest in the world and all the people I don't like are forced to build me a castle in France."

Stephanie Vanderkellen,
Newhart

❖

"Having a dream isn't stupid, Norm. It's not having a dream that's stupid."

Cliff Clavin,
Cheers

❖

"If dreaming is all your subconscious desires coming out, why do people wait 'til they're asleep to do it?"

Max Headroom,
Max Headroom

❖

Gorgeous Woman [longingly]: "About that dream you had. . . . "
Bruce Wayne: "Do we dare?"
Woman: "Why not?"
Wayne [looking guilty]: "Yes, of course . . . why not? Of what use is a dream . . . if not a blueprint for courageous action?"

Batman

❖

"The wild dreams of today are the practical realities of tomorrow."
Captain Crane,
Voyage to the Bottom of the Sea

Earth

"We may make all sorts of blunders, wander off the path now and then, but ultimately we belong where we belong . . . on Earth."
Prof. Victor Bergman,
Space: 1999

❖

"The planet Earth is a speck of dust, remote and alone in the void. There are powers in the universe inscrutable and profound. Fear cannot save us. Rage cannot help us. We must see the stranger in a new light—the light of understanding. And to achieve this, we must begin to understand ourselves and each other."
The Control Voice,
The Outer Limits

❖

Morticia Addams: "Darling, you know so much about the world."
Gomez Addams: "I've lived in it all my life."
The Addams Family

❖

"Earth's all right for a visit, but I wouldn't want to live here."
Uncle Martin,
My Favorite Martian

❖

"Earth! You can't be serious. That's nothing but a fable!"
Count Baltar,
Battlestar Galactica

Eating

Aunt Bee: "Did you like the white beans you had for supper?"
Andy Taylor: "Um hmm."
Bee: "Well, you didn't say anything."
Andy: "Well, I ate four bowls. If that ain't a tribute to white beans, I
   don't know what is."
Bee: "Well. . . . "
Andy: "Eating speaks louder than words."

The Andy Griffith Show

❖

Florence: "Is there something you don't like about my cooking?"
George Jefferson: "Yeah—eating it."

The Jeffersons

❖

Joanie Cunningham: "Barbara Jo Allen ate a fly."
Howard Cunningham: "Well, with beef at sixty-eight cents a pound,
   I don't blame her."

Happy Days

❖

"When a person eats fluffy eats, little cakes, pastry, and fancy little things, then that person is also fluffy. But when you eat meats and strong, heavy food, then you are also a strong person."

Dr. Kurt von Stuffer (Sid Caesar),
Your Show of Shows

❖

Guardian: "Hog jowls, possum pie! Do you intend to feed those things to Master Armstrong?"
Jed Clampett: "Why? Don't he eat that good at home?"

The Beverly Hillbillies

❖

Felix Unger: "Do you always talk with your mouth full?"
Oscar Madison: "Only when I'm eating."

The Odd Couple

❖

"Did you ever play, 'Let's see if this is edible'?"

Larry,
Newhart

❖

"The way prices are going up is a disgrace. Pretty soon indigestion is going to be a luxury."

Martha Shumway,
Mary Hartman, Mary Hartman

❖

"Why am I bothering to eat this chocolate? I might as well apply it directly to my thighs."

Rhoda Morgenstern,
The Mary Tyler Moore Show

❖

"It ain't over till the fat lady eats."

Balki Bartokomous,
Perfect Strangers

Elvis

"He's that fella we see every now and then on television, shakin' and screamin' kinda like somebody's beatin' his dog."

Sheriff Andy Taylor,
The Andy Griffith Show

❖

Groucho Marx: "Are you interested in matrimony?"
Fan Club President: "Indeed I am."
Groucho: "Do you have any other interests?"
Fan Club President: "You haven't mentioned Elvis Presley."
Groucho: "I seldom do unless I stub my toe."

You Bet Your Life

Embarrassment

Groucho Marx: "You don't mind if I ask you a few personal questions, do you?"
Model: "If they're not too embarrassing."
Groucho: "Don't give it a second thought. I've asked thousands of questions on this show and I've yet to be embarrassed."

You Bet Your Life

❖

Judge: "Maverick, I guess you're about the only man in the world who'd be insulted if somebody called him a good man."
Bret Maverick: "Not insulted—embarrassed."

Maverick

Enemies

"Respect your enemies, boys. Good enemies make good armies."

Cattleman,
Gunsmoke

❖

"When you know an enemy's strengths, and can use them against them, they become weaknesses."

Servalan,
Blake's 7

❖

Will Robinson: "Well, if you are going to be such a great ruler, you should try and understand others. Even your enemies."
Megazor: "I do understand my enemies. They all want to kill me."

Lost in Space

Ethnic Remarks

"I am *not* a minority. I'm an outnumbered majority."

Ed Brown,
Chico and the Man

❖

"Have you always been a Negro, or are you just trying to be fashionable?"

Dr. Morton Chesley,
Julia

❖

Mike Stivic: "Arch, if there's no personal contact, there's no danger of further infection."
Archie Bunker: "That's with regular germs. But them Polack bugs

you got may be too dumb to know the rules and regulations. And if those germs of yours got any sense of all, they're poppin' out of you right now, lookin' for a better home."

All in the Family

❖

"I can't eat that Chink food; those people do their cooking and their laundry in the same pot."

Fred Sanford,
Sanford and Son

❖

"Jesus was a Jew, yes, but only on his mother's side."

Archie Bunker,
All in the Family

❖

"We don't get pimples. God said, 'I'll just screw up their hair.'"

Benson,
Soap

❖

L.P.: "She's from one of California's first families."
Chico Rodriguez: "Oh, is she Mexican too?"

Chico and the Man

❖

Howard Hunter: "I was wondering if I could ask you a direct and personal question?"
Henry Goldblume: "Sure. Fire away."
Howard: "What is it like being a Hebrew?"

Hill Street Blues

❖

"Boy, was this apartment dirty! It's guys like you that give Caucasians a bad name."

Ernie Reyes,
Sidekicks

❖

Det. Ron Harris: "Remember, there's an old Chinese proverb: Save a
man's life and he'll never forgive you."
Mr. Deluca: "That doesn't make sense."
Harris: "Hey, *I'm* not Chinese. . . . [thoughtfully, to himself] They're
supposed to be damned clever."

Barney Miller

Evil

The Joker: "Have you any last words, Caped Crusader?"
Batman: "Just this, Joker—evil sometimes triumphs temporarily . . .
but never conquers."

Batman

❖

"Without that deadly talent for being in the right place at the right
time, evil must suffer defeat. And with each defeat, Doomsday is
postponed . . . for at least one more day."

The Control Voice,
The Outer Limits

"Spock . . . I've found that evil usually triumphs—unless good is very,
very careful."

Dr. Leonard McCoy,
Star Trek

❖

"There are no holidays in the fight against evil."

Maxwell Smart,
Get Smart

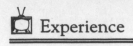
Experience

"A fellow has a dream and he goes after it . . . It doesn't work, he comes back. A fellow like that's kinda lived a little, you know."

Sheriff Andy Taylor,
The Andy Griffith Show

❖

"You really are naive! You've got to start watching soap operas."

Quincy,
Quincy

❖

"Inexperience is not inability, and you can do anything you believe you can."

Illya Kuryakin,
The Man from U.N.C.L.E.

"I'm an experienced woman; I've been around. . . . Well, all right, I might not've been around, but I've been . . . nearby."

Mary Richards,
The Mary Tyler Moore Show

❖

"It's merely the difference of a few years, old chum. An older head can't be put on younger shoulders."

Batman,
Batman

The Facts of Life

"I guess there's two things that'll always be in the world—dirt and homework."

Ward Cleaver,
Leave It to Beaver

❖

"To be complacent is to be but one step from decay."

Gilt Proto,
Lost in Space

❖

"Regret is part of being alive."

Kerr Avon,
Blake's 7

❖

"Desperation tends to make one flexible."

MacGyver,
MacGyver

❖

"Flattery is the floating cockroach in the milk of human kindness."

Twiggy Rathbone,
Hot Metal

❖

"The power to hope cannot be taken away with a gun or fences."

Caine,
Kung Fu

❖

"The secret of survival is: Always expect the unexpected."

Doctor Who,
Doctor Who

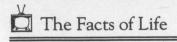
❖

"Reservations are the condoms in the birth of new ideas."

Twiggy Rathbone,
Hot Metal

❖

"Boredom, like necessity, is very often the mother of invention."

Dr. Smith,
Lost in Space

❖

"There's two ways for a fellow to look for adventure: By tearing everything down or building everything up."

Jim Haskel,
The Lone Ranger

❖

"There are three things you don't get over in a hurry—losing a woman, eating bad possum, and eating good possum."

Beau La Barre,
Welcome Back, Kotter

❖

"Asking is just polite demanding."

Max Headroom,
Max Headroom

❖

"My pa always says that understandin' is like a gold coin—there are two sides."

Israel Boone,
Daniel Boone

❖

Captain Kirk: "There are a million things in this universe you can have, and there are a million things you can't have. It's no fun

facing that, but that's the way things are."
Charlie: "Well, then what am I going to do?"
Kirk: "Hang on tight . . . and survive. Everybody does."

Star Trek

❖

"There's an old Moroccan saying—trust in God, but tie your camel tight."

Annie McGuire,
Annie McGuire

Faith

"To me, Stevens, the most important ingredient of a product is the pride of the man who makes it. Of all the pet foods we manufacture, my favorite is our birdseed. Now, I *believe* in birdseed."

Mr. Springer,
Bewitched

❖

"I do believe in Santa Claus . . . *that's* one thing I believe in."

Cindy, age 4,
Candid Camera

❖

"Son, when a man knows something deep down in his heart . . . when he really knows . . . he doesn't have to argue about it, doesn't have to prove it. Just knowin', that's enough."

Ben Cartwright,
Bonanza

Det. Stanley Wojohowicz [booking prostitute]: "Any previous convictions?"
Hooker: "Yeah, I once thought cleanliness was next to godliness."
Barney Miller

❖

"All faith must have a little doubt mixed in. . . . Otherwise it's just flabby sentimentality."

Dr. Loveless,
The Wild, Wild West

Family

"Whatever trouble he's in, his family has the right to share it with him. It's our duty to help him if we can and it's his duty to let us and he doesn't have the privilege to change that."

Jarrod Barkley,
The Big Valley

❖

[To his sister] "Eunice, I'm worried that insanity is hereditary. . . . I mean, our sister marries a priest, Dad's a murderer, Grandpa's still fighting World War II, and Mom lives on Mars. . . . We're next!"

Billy Tate,
Soap

❖

"Don't allow no weirdos on the phone unless it's family."

Mama Harper,
Mama's Family

❖

"Her origins are so low, you'd have to limbo under her family tree."

Minister,
SCTV

❖

"The first rule of orphanages and Irish families is there's always room for one more."

Father Francis Mulcahy,
M*A*S*H

❖

"If you're gonna steal, steal from kin—at least they're less likely to put the law on you."

Bret Maverick,
Maverick

Fashion

"I wonder why everyone dressed old-fashioned in those days. They don't do it now."

Kathy Anderson,
Father Knows Best

❖

"There's something neat about a sweater with a hole. It makes you look like a tough guy."

Beaver Cleaver,
Leave It to Beaver

❖

"If women dressed for men, the stores wouldn't sell much—just an occasional sun visor."

Groucho Marx,
You Bet Your Life

❖

"It's amazing what a new dress will do for a girl's spirits."

Miss Kitty,
Gunsmoke

❖

Florence Johnston [wearing a bright red dress]: "Do you think this color suits me?"
George Jefferson: "Sure—it's loud, isn't it?"

The Jeffersons

Fat

"I love my blubber. It keeps me warm, it keeps me company, it keeps my pants up."

Oscar Madison,
The Odd Couple

❖

"He's not fat, he's just short for his weight."

Endora,
Bewitched

❖

Ralph Kramden [into a new scheme]: "This is probably the biggest thing I ever got into."
Alice Kramden: "The biggest thing you ever got into was your pants."

The Honeymooners

❖

Peter Marshall (the emcee): "Jackie Gleason recently revealed that he firmly believes in them and has actually seen them on at least two occasions. What are they?"
Charlie Weaver: "His feet."

Hollywood Squares

Fathers

"The only fathers that don't yell at their kids are on television."

Wally Cleaver,
Leave It to Beaver

❖

"Daddies make the best friends. Why do you think dogs always hang out with them?"

Cliff Huxtable,
The Cosby Show

❖

"There are no bad children, there are only stingy fathers."

Davey Gillis,
The Many Loves of Dobie Gillis

❖

"Being a father is something that lives in your heart and grows over a long period of time."

Starman,
Starman

❖

Ben Cartwright: "I'm not in the habit of giving lectures, and if I do, it's because they're needed. Might have been a good idea if your father had given you a few."
Candy Canaday: "Oh, he did."
Ben: "Obviously they didn't have much effect."
Candy: "Oh, yes they did; I left home."

Bonanza

❖

"I am your father. I brought you into this world and I can take you out."

Cliff Huxtable,
The Cosby Show

❖

"Dad always said hi to our friends, but it was like he had this understanding with the family: He worked hard for us, he provided for us, and he certainly didn't want to have to talk to us on top of that. My approach was to not make any sudden moves or sounds until he'd finished that first vodka tonic and hope that nobody else did anything else that might upset him too much until then."

Kevin Arnold,
The Wonder Years

Fear

"When fear is too terrible, when reality is too agonizing, we seek escape in manufactured danger, in the thrills and pleasures of pretending—in the amusement parks of our unamusing world. Here, in frantic pretending, Man finds escape and temporary peace, and goes home tired enough to sleep a short, deep sleep."

The Control Voice,
The Outer Limits

❖

"I'm always worried about people who aren't scared when they ought to be."

Illya Kuryakin,
The Man from U.N.C.L.E.

❖

Caine: "Of all things, to live in darkness must be the worst."
Master Po: "Fear is the only darkness."

Kung Fu

❖

"The subject: fear. The cure: a little more faith. An Rx off a shelf—in the Twilight Zone."

Rod Serling,
The Twilight Zone

❖

"Every man gets scared once or twice in his life—unless he's stupid."
Ben Calhoun,
Iron Horse

❖

"Anxiety magnifies fearsome objects."

Barney Fife,
The Andy Griffith Show

❖

"I don't like being afraid. It scares me."
Margaret "Hot Lips" Houlihan,
M*A*S*H

❖

"Some people are afraid of the dark and some are afraid to leave it."
Beau Maverick,
Maverick

Food

"The first thing I remember liking that liked me back was food."
Rhoda Morgenstern Gerard,
Rhoda

❖

"That's your idea of a romantic dinner, Oscar? Red wine and fish
sticks?"

Felix Unger,
The Odd Couple

❖

"Radar, don't pick at your food; it won't heal."

Hawkeye Pierce,
M*A*S*H

❖

Gary Levy: "Do you have any food I could eat?"
Rhoda Morgenstern: "As opposed to food you could wear?"
The Mary Tyler Moore Show

❖

"This recipe is certainly silly. It says to separate two eggs, but it doesn't say how far to separate them."

Gracie Allen,
The George Burns and Gracie Allen Show

Gracie Allen: "Every time I bake a cake I leave it in five minutes too long and it burns."
Harry Von Zell: "So?"
Gracie: "So, today I put in one cake, and I put in another five minutes later. When the first one starts to burn, I'll know the second one's finished."
The George Burns and Gracie Allen Show

❖

Oscar Madison: "You want brown juice or green juice?"
Felix Unger: "What's the difference?"
Oscar: "Two weeks."

The Odd Couple

❖

John Burns: "I try to eat only natural things."
Louie DePalma: "How'd you like a sack of dirt?"

Taxi

❖

"If you are ever served a rare steak that is intended for somebody else, don't bother with ethical details. Eat as much as you can before the mistake is discovered."

Pappy Maverick,
Maverick

❖

"What vegetable would your husband most like to sit on?"

Bob Eubanks,
The Newlywed Game

❖

Rocky Rockford: "Hot dogs again?"
Jim Rockford: "Just try to think of them as tube steaks."
The Rockford Files

❖

Felix: "Candy and soda for breakfast?"
Oscar: "Candy and soda are energy foods."
The Odd Couple

Amos McCoy: "Just take a whiff of that soup she's makin' . . . um-um."
Kate McCoy: "I'm boilin' Little Luke's overalls. . . . "
Amos: "How do you like that? She makes *everything* smell good."
The Real McCoys

❖

"I picked up a few 'Saturday night is the loneliest night of the week' carbohydrates. There was a special on cheese spread. And Ding-Dongs. I guess I could put some cheese spread on them."

Judy,
The Slap Maxwell Story

Food for Thought

"Time is an illusion. Lunchtime doubly so."

Ford Prefect,
The Hitchhiker's Guide to the Galaxy

❖

"Can you imagine a roast aardvark without an apple in its mouth? It's like a martini without the egg."

Gomez Addams,
The Addams Family

❖

"Jedediah, sometimes you have to wade through the hogwallow to get to the melons."

Barnaby Jones,
Barnaby Jones

❖

"Exploding meatballs always ruin my appetite."

Matthew Star,
The Powers of Matthew Star

❖

Rocky: "Hey, Bullwinkle. Did you read where Adler Suggins went over Niagara Falls on a bagel?"
Bullwinkle: "That's pretty amazing."
Rocky: "Yeah."
Bullwinkle: "I didn't think they made those big bagels any more."
The Rocky and Bullwinkle Show

Food: What Goes Down Must Come Up

Cpl. Klinger: "Lunchtime, folks. Grab your platter and watch it splatter. . . . Have some stew, Colonel?"

Col. Potter: "What kind is it?"

Klinger: "Could be beef, pork, or water buffalo. [Confidentially] We'll never know and it won't tell."

Potter: "Well, as long as it's dead. Spoon it on, son . . . no toast."

Klinger [to co-server]: One brown puddle, hold the shingle."

M*A*S*H*

❖

Allen Funt [to little girl]: "Carol, what do you eat for breakfast?"

Carol: "Sometimes hot dogs, sometimes potatoes."

Funt: "No orange juice in the morning?"

Carol: "Oh yes—and hot dogs."

Funt: "Cereal?"

Carol: "Yes, and hot dogs."

Funt: "And for dinner?"

Carol: "Hot dogs."

Funt: "And after dinner, Carol, do you go to sleep right away?"

Carol: "No. . . . First I throw up."

Candid Camera

❖

Art Linkletter: "What do you think of the saying, 'The early bird gets the worm'?"

Kid: "He's welcome to it. I tried it once and it tasted like cold spaghetti."

Art Linkletter's House Party

Freedom

"To seek freedom, a man must struggle. To win it, he must choose wisely where and when he struggles, or it is like spitting in the wind."

Caine,
Kung Fu

❖

"Freedom's got a lot to do with what you've got in your pocket, and I've got about eighty-five cents."

Bret Maverick,
Maverick

Free Enterprise

"You can't make one thin dime giving people what they need. You've got to give 'em what they want."

Angel Martin,
The Rockford Files

❖

Oliver Wendell Douglas: "Mr. Haney, I'm warning you—I'm about fed up with your schemes. One of these days you're going to go too far, and when that day comes, I'm going to help nail you."
Mr. Haney: "Would you care to buy a hammer?"

Green Acres

❖

Pilar Ortega: "I never mix business with pleasure."
Lance Cumson: "You haven't done business with *me*."

Falcon Crest

❖

[Describing the ideal ad executive]
"He's hard-working, he's not impressed by facts, he's slippery, he lies beautifully, and he's got a nice head of hair."

McMann,
Bewitched

❖

"We make money the old-fashioned way—we borrow it."

A stockbroker,
Barney Miller

Freeways

Uncle Fester: "They're going to build a freeway."
Gomez Addams: "A freeway through our fair city?"
Morticia Addams: "Well, a freeway may have its compensations. There's something rather musical about the sound of crunching metal."

The Addams Family

Friends

"My pa always said every man was your friend until he shows you otherwise."

Hoss,
Bonanza

❖

"You're nothing but a tiny dot, a speck, a minute insignificant nothing. But I'm proud to call you my friend."

Warren Ferguson,
The Andy Griffith Show

❖

"Anyone who can't keep a secret can't keep a friend."

Uncle Martin,
My Favorite Martian

❖

"A friend, I am told, is worth more than pure gold."

Popeye,
The Popeye Cartoon Show

❖

"I've never felt closer to a group of people. Not even in the portable johns of Woodstock."

Reverend Jim Ignatowski,
Taxi

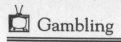
❖

"Y'know, when we're not fighting, we get along just fine."

Val Pointer,
The Rockford Files

❖

"Through the years we'll all be friends, wherever we may be.
M–I–C–K–E–Y, M–O–U–S–E."

The Mouseketeers,
The Mickey Mouse Club

Gambling

"A sucker's groan is music to a gambler's ear."

Sgt. Bilko,
The Phil Silvers Show

❖

"Don't gamble unless you have to, but if you have to, go for broke."

Doug Phillips,
The Time Tunnel

❖

"There's no such thing as a sure thing. That's why they call it gambling."

Oscar Madison,
The Odd Couple

❖

"Where would Al Capone be today if he didn't take chances?"

Sgt. Bilko,
The Phil Silvers Show

❖

"Son, the best time to get 'lucky' is when the other man's dealing."
Pappy Maverick,
Maverick

❖

"Stay out of poker games where you don't know the stakes."
Ben Cartwright,
Bonanza

God

"God don't make no mistakes—that's how he got to be God."
Archie Bunker,
All in the Family

❖

Archie Bunker: "All the pictures I ever seen, God is white."
George Jefferson: "Maybe you were looking at the negatives."
All in the Family

❖

"Well, I certainly don't believe God's a woman, because if He were, men would be the ones walking around wearing high heels, taking Midol, and having their upper lips waxed."
Julia Sugarbaker,
Designing Women

❖

"I'm a scientist—I don't know anything about God."
Prof. Victor Bergman,
Space: 1999

❖

"God is just a name for . . . God."

Cmdr. John Koenig,
Space: 1999

❖

"It's funny the way some people's name just suits the business they're in. Like God's name is just *perfect* for God."

Edith Bunker,
All in the Family

❖

Gabe Kotter: "I think God is everywhere."
Arnold Horschack: "Even in liver?"

Welcome Back, Kotter

❖

"When I was dead I saw God. She looks just like Toody from 'The Facts of Life.' "

Larry,
Newhart

❖

"Sometimes it seems like we're a needle that's stuck in the bad-luck groove of the record of life. But you'll see. God's gonna come along and just nudge us back on track any day now."

Loretta Haggars,
Mary Hartman, Mary Hartman

❖

"Many a time we've been down to our last piece of fatback. And I'd say, 'Should we eat it or render it down for soap?' Your Uncle Jed would say, 'Render it down. God will provide food for us poor folks, but we gotta do our own washin'.' "

Granny,
The Beverly Hillbillies

The Golden Years

"Most of us, by the time we're up on the rules, are generally too old to play."

Pappy Maverick,
Maverick

❖

"You know, Dorothy, people think if you live to be my age, you should be grateful just to be alive. Well, that's not how it works. You need a reason to get up in the morning, and sometimes even after you find one, life can turn right around and spit in your face."

Sophia,
The Golden Girls

❖

Groucho Marx: "Are you married, Bill?"
Bill: "No, I'm separated."
Groucho: "When a man gets to be your age, you have to expect to start coming apart. Maybe you've been using the wrong kind of glue."

You Bet Your Life

❖

"If you make it to one hundred that fat weather guy will announce your name on TV."

George Utley,
Newhart

❖

"What do you think I do all day? I sit. I walk. . . . Sometimes I lean. What else can I do? Doctors found all this stuff to keep us going for ninety years, but we ain't got anyplace to go. . . ."

Grandpa Larkin,
Mary Hartman, Mary Hartman

❖

Granny: "Why don' y' just shoot me like an ol' horse an' sell m' body fer glue?"

Jed Clampett: "Now, Granny, that's ridiculous."
Jethro Bodine: "Yeah, you wouldn't make enough glue fer a—"
Jed: "Don't help me, boy!"

The Beverly Hillbillies

Golf

"We're playing a game where the aim is to be below par. It's so wrong for me."

Stephanie Vanderkellen,
Newhart

❖

Janitor: "Are you a golfer?"
Professor Kingsfield: "No, I'm afraid I lack the temperament
   required to chase a little ball over acres of what should be animal
   pasture."

The Paper Chase

❖

Jed Clampett: "We're gonna be shooting some game called golf."
Granny: "What in tarnation is a golf?"
Jed: "I don't know, but they must be thicker'n crows in a corn patch
   around here because everybody in Beverly Hills shoots 'em."
Granny: "Never seen 'em around. They must live in holes in the
   ground like a gopher."
Jed: "Reckon maybe you're right. Mr. Drysdale says he shot nine
   holes of golf and got fifty-seven."

The Beverly Hillbillies

Good Looks

"You know, it *eez* possible to be too attractive."

Pepe Le Pew,
The Bugs Bunny Show

"Listen McGarrett, I don't look good when I bleed."

> Joey Lee,
> *Hawaii Five-0*

❖

"Good looks are no substitute for a sound character."

> Doctor Who,
> *Doctor Who*

❖

"What kind of world is it where ugliness is the norm and beauty the deviation from that norm? The answer is, it doesn't make any difference. Because the old saying happens to be true. Beauty *is* in the eye of the beholder, in this year or a hundred years hence, on this planet or wherever there is human life, perhaps out among the stars. Beauty is in the eye of the beholder. Lesson to be learned . . . in the Twilight Zone."

> Rod Serling,
> *The Twilight Zone*

❖

"May I say you're looking as appetizing as a truck-struck weasel."

> Larry,
> *Newhart*

Good Samaritans

New Yorker (victim): "Lemme get this straight—you're saying that you saw me in trouble, so you came over for no reason, with nothing in it for you, and saved my life."
Good Samaritan: "Yep."
Victim: "You're sick!"

> *Barney Miller*

❖

"Remember, it's better to give—than to get five across your lips."

> Fred Sanford,
> *Sanford and Son*

❖

Kristin: "You want me to sell myself so I can spy on your friends. Is that it?"

J.R. Ewing: "Well, you're always saying you want to help."

Dallas

Gossip

"What is whispered in the ear is heard miles away. And that tells us that we must always guard our tongues against gossip. . . . We must never make idle or careless remarks that reflect on the honesty or character of anyone."

Jimmie Dodd,
The Mickey Mouse Club

❖

"Enquiring minds want to know."

Ad for the *National Enquirer*

Grandparents

"You can't get in trouble with grandparents. All you have to do is kiss them when they come in the door, tell them you miss them, let them buy you stuff—you're okay!"

Alex Keaton,
Family Ties

Greatness

"The great ones are never understood in their own lifetime."

Slap Maxwell,
The Slap Maxwell Story

"Greatness is like Spam—it never goes bad."

Dora,
I Married Dora

Greed

"Oh, yes indeedy, it doesn't pay to be greedy."

Popeye,
The Popeye Cartoon Show

❖

Robin [anguished]: "The Bat-diamond!"
Batman: "What about it, Robin?"
Robin: "To think it's the cause of all this trouble!"
Batman: "People call it many things, old chum: passion, lust, desire, avarice. . . . But the simplest and most understandable word is *greed*."

Batman

❖

"I have a good reason for robbing the bank. I love money!"

Crook,
Atom Ant

❖

Darrin Stevens: "Larry, do you know when you talk about money your eyes light up?"
Larry Tate: "Of course. I'm a greedy person."

Bewitched

❖

Rick Simon: "I kind of like the guy."
A.J. Simon: "That's because he's giving you money. You like anyone who gives you money. I think you were a hooker in another life."

Simon and Simon

Greens

"Ya has nothing to fear when spinach is near."

Popeye,
The Popeye Cartoon Show

❖

Mork: "Do you have anything green in the icebox?"
Mindy McConnell: "Last month's cottage cheese."
Mork: "Well, leafy green is better than lumpy green, but I'll give
  it a try."

Mork and Mindy

Growing Up

"You don't need any brains to grow up. It just happens to ya."

Gilbert,
Leave It to Beaver

❖

"What's the use of growing up if you can't act childish sometimes?"

Doctor Who,
Doctor Who

❖

"Growing up doesn't have to be so much a
straight line as a series of advances."

Kevin Arnold,
The Wonder Years

❖

Robin [gazing at a female criminal's legs]:
  "Her legs sort of remind me of
  Catwoman's."
Batman: "You're growing up, Robin. But
  remember: In crimefighting, always
  keep your sights high."

Batman

Guilt

"Joe, never feel guilty about having warm human feelings toward anyone."

Ben Cartwright,
Bonanza

❖

"The Sweathog motto: Whatever it is, I didn't do it."

Freddie Washington,
Welcome Back, Kotter

❖

"Lily! Lily! The world's coming to an end and it's all my fault."

Herman Munster,
The Munsters

❖

Blanche Fedders: "You must be a very informed person, Mary. Who else would know so much about Jewish people and chicken soup?"
Mary Hartman: "Well . . . most guilty people would."

Mary Hartman, Mary Hartman

Guns

"When a man carries a gun all the time, the respect he thinks he's getting might really be fear. So I don't carry a gun because I don't want the people of Mayberry to fear a gun; I'd rather they would respect me."

Sheriff Andy Taylor,
The Andy Griffith Show

❖

"Would you mind turning around so I can shoot you in the back?"

Uncle Fester,
The Addams Family

[Rockford takes out a gun]
Client: "I thought you didn't like to shoot people."
Jim Rockford: "I don't shoot it. I just point it."

The Rockford Files

❖

Alfred: "I don't know much about guns."
Remington: "Oh, they're very overrated. You just point them away
from you and shoot."

Remington Steele

❖

"A gun is not a tool for peace."

Caine,
Kung Fu

❖

"Using another man's gun is like eating with another man's teeth."
Ben Maverick,
Maverick

❖

"If I had time to clean up the mess, I'd shoot you."

J.R. Ewing,
Dallas

❖

Archie Bunker: "Did you ever think of takin' a shot at me, Edith?"
Edith Bunker: "No."
Archie: "That's good. And I never wanted to shoot you neither. It's
nice when people get along together. Right, Edith?"

All in the Family

The Halls of Justice

Alex Reiger: "Louie, when you walk into that hearing room, you're
going to be under oath. You know what that means?"
Louie DePalma: "Yeah. It means they gotta believe you. I love this
country."

Taxi

❖

Venus Flytrap: "I'm not gonna sit here and let her lie!"
Lawyer: "You have to. This is a court of law."

WKRP in Cincinnati

❖

"Cross-examination is like making love—it's so much better when
you're not interrupted."

Horace Rumpole,
Rumpole of the Bailey

❖

Jim Anderson: "Going to court isn't something to be ashamed of."
Kathy Anderson: "Heck no. Judges go all the time."

Father Knows Best

❖

Gomez Addams: "I've gone through the city ordinances, the Bill of
Rights, and the seventeen volumes of assorted jurisprudence—and
I've come to a conclusion."
Morticia Addams: "What?"

Gomez: "That we haven't got a leg to stand on."
Uncle Fester: "Not even if we bribe the judge?"

The Addams Family

❖

"This is America. You can't make a horse testify against himself."

Mr. Ed,
Mr. Ed

Health

Doctor: "Did your parents enjoy good health?"
Gracie Allen: "Oh yes, they loved it."

The George Burns and Gracie Allen Show

❖

"She was in perfect condition except for one thing—she's dead."

Quincy,
Quincy

❖

"In the world of ulcers, Unger, you're what's known as a carrier."

Dr. Gordon,
The Odd Couple

❖

Larry Appleton: "What you've got is a classic case of insomnia."
Balki Bartokomous: "Oh, no. . . . I knew it was something terrible!
  Okay, give it to me straight. How long have I got?"
Larry: "Fifty or sixty years."
Balki: "Fifty or sixty years? Oh, my God, a slow death!"

Perfect Strangers

Heaven

"You don't have to be homely to get into heaven."

Hattie Denton,
The Rifleman

❖

Jean-Paul Sartre [arriving in heaven]: "It's not what I expected."
God: "What did you expect?"
Sartre: "Nothing."

SCTV

❖

"There's no plea bargaining in heaven."

Mark McCormick,
Hardcastle and McCormick

Heroes

"Heroes take chances."

Ralph Hinckley,
The Greatest American Hero

❖

"Look at him! He's willing to stay here and face the killer single handed! He's ready to give up his life! He's not afraid to die! He don't mind if he ends up with a bullet in his head! He *wants* to die! He *wants* to lie there in the gutter! He *knows* he hasn't a chance! He *knows* they'll shoot him down like a dog! But he doesn't care. He's an idiot! And I'm getting out of town before it's too late."

Imogene Coca,
Your Show of Shows

❖

"Superheroes get free donuts."

Mighty Mouse,
The New Adventures of Mighty Mouse

❖

Natasha Fatale [pretending to cry]: "Boo-Hoo."
Rocket J. Squirrel [walking near her]: "Hold it, Bullwinkle. That

sounds like a lady in distress."

Bullwinkle Moose: "So?"

Rocky: "Gee, didn't you ever read *The Hero's Handbook?*"

Bullwinkle: "I could never get past the picture of General MacArthur on the cover."

Rocky: "Well, chapter two says we should always help ladies in distress."

Bullwinkle [to Natasha]: "Hi there. Are you in distress?"

Natasha: "Dis dress, dat dress....Who cares? I'm distraught."

Bullwinkle [looking in book]: "Do we help ladies in distraught?"

The Bullwinkle Show

❖

"Boys don't have many heroes left that they can look up to these days. If I let Eddie down, all he has left is Smokey the Bear."

Herman Munster,
The Munsters

❖

Gomez Addams: "Gee, perhaps we really *have* saved the world?"

Morticia Addams: "Oh, darling—do you think we did the right thing?"

The Addams Family

Higher Education

"Look, I've been going to school all my life. You can't get in trouble by keeping your mouth shut."

Wally Cleaver,
Leave It to Beaver

❖

School Principal: "I'm sure your children will be very happy here."

Gomez: "If we'd wanted them to be happy, we would've let them stay at home."

The Addams Family

❖

"A suburban junior high school cafeteria is like a microcosm of the world. The goal is to protect yourself, and safety comes in groups. You had your cool kids, you had your smart kids, you had your greasers. And in those days, of course, you had your hippies. In effect, in junior high school, who you are is defined less by who you are than who is the person next to you."

Kevin Arnold,
The Wonder Years

❖

"Y'know what I hate about the first day of school? It's too far from the last day of school."

Freddie Washington,
Welcome Back, Kotter

❖

"Next week I have to take my college aptitude test. In my high school they didn't even *teach* aptitude."

Tony Banta,
Taxi

❖

"I'm taking mathematics at school. I hate it! You take most of the trouble in the world today. . . . What's behind it? Math, that's what. I mean, without math, there wouldn't be H-bombs or income tax or insufficient funds at the bank."

Dobie Gillis,
The Many Loves of Dobie Gillis

❖

Sondra Huxtable: "Mom, I'm not going to law school. . . . "
Claire Huxtable: "Sondra, what are you saying? You have always wanted to go to law school. You've never talked about anything else."
Sondra: "I've changed my mind."
Claire: "After all the money we spent sending you to Princeton? Sondra, you owe us $79,648.22, and I want my money . . . NOW."
The Cosby Show

❖

"Sometimes I just wish I were Ozzie Nelson. He'd just say, 'Go to college'—and that would be the end of that."

Howard Cunningham,
Happy Days

❖

"You don't measure a college by the courses they give you. It's by the fraternities. Look, pay attention . . . You guys can graduate with your Ph.D.'s, your B.A.'s, whatever, but just let me get next to a fraternity brother whose old man is the president of some oil company, and I got it made."

Eddie Haskell,
Leave It to Beaver

History

"What could be more fun than history? The chills, the spills, the splendor of it all!"

Pee-Wee Herman,
Pee-Wee's Playhouse

❖

"Here on the 'Bullwinkle Show,' we believe in history. . . . 'Cause history means progress . . . and if it wasn't for progress, where would one be today? On radio, that's where."

Bullwinkle J. Moose,
The Bullwinkle Show

❖

"Every thinking pioneer and inventor has suffered the same kind of ridicule. It's right there in your history books. . . . Take Alexander Graham Bell. People laughed at him right over the telephone. Wilbur and Orville. Practically laughed them off Wright Air Force Base. People have to be shown."

Barney Fife,
The Andy Griffith Show

❖

"History is mostly killin' people."

> Beaver Cleaver,
> *Leave It to Beaver*

❖

"You can't rewrite history—not one line!"

> Doctor Who,
> *Doctor Who*

❖

Larry Appleton: "This must have been how Eisenhower felt just before D-Day. All around him, the troops sleeping; not Ike! He knew that one single mistake could change the course of world history."
Balki Bartokomous: "Was this before or after Ike met Tina Turner?"

> *Perfect Strangers*

Home

Colonel: "Is that all you do, loiter around gambling houses?"
Beau Maverick: "Home is where the heart is."

> *Maverick*

❖

"What a picture of domestic tranquility. . . . Hemlock on the hearth and my wife feeding the piranha."

> Gomez Addams,
> *The Addams Family*

❖

Jed Clampett: "Pearl, what d'ya think? Think I oughta move?"
Cousin Pearl: "Jed, how can ya even ask? Look around ya. You're eight miles from yore nearest neighbor. Yore overrun with skunks, possums, coyotes, bobcats. You use kerosene lamps fer light and you cook on a wood stove summer and winter. Yore drinkin' homemade moonshine and washin' with homemade lye soap. And

yore bathroom is fifty feet from the house and you ask 'should I move?' "

Jed: "I reckon yore right. A man'd be a dang fool to leave all this!"

The Beverly Hillbillies

❖

"Home is where the computer is."

Felix the Cat,
The Adventures of Felix the Cat

❖

"You put up with a few inconveniences when you live in a condemned building."

Reverend Jim Ignatowski,
Taxi

Home Improvement

"When rolling out the fiberglass it is very important that you wear gloves, or you might add insulation to injury."

Dick Loudon,
Newhart

❖

Balki Bartokomous: "I just know you're doing it the wrong way. What did the directions say?"

Larry Appleton: "Directions? I threw them out. My father has made it through his whole life without ever reading a set of directions. He once rewired the entire house without directions."

Balki: "Isn't that the house that burned to the ground?"

Larry: "They never proved it was the wiring."

Perfect Strangers

❖

George Burns: "What's that?"

Gracie Allen: "Electric cords. I had them shortened. This one's for the iron, this one's for the floor lamp."

George: "Why did you shorten them?"
Gracie: "To save electricity."

The George Burns and Gracie Allen Show

Homosexual Panic

Danny Williams: "What did your fortune cookie say, Steve?"
Steve McGarrett: "It said, 'A beautiful blond woman will soon come into your life.' Fat chance."
Danny: "Want to trade? Mine said, 'You will soon meet a tall, dark, handsome man.' "
Steve: "Too bad, Danno."

Hawaii Five-0

❖

"It's only common sense. If God wanted people to be gay, he wouldn't have created Adam and Eve—he would have created Adam and Steve."

Arthur Harmon,
Maude

Honesty

"I think honesty is usually the best policy here in these United States of America."

Molly Dodd,
The Days and Nights of Molly Dodd

❖

Jason: "I want to thank you, Mr. DeWitt, for letting Mike take this make-up test."
Mr. DeWitt: "No problem."
Jason: "I think he's learned now that intending to cheat was just as bad as cheating itself."
Mr. DeWitt: "That's what my ex-wife said in court."

Growing Pains

❖

"Honesty is the best policy and spinach is the best vegetable."

Popeye,
The Popeye Cartoon Show

❖

"Since we're into honesty, let me tell you that your normal voice sounds like Truman Capote on helium."

Mindy McConnell,
Mork and Mindy

Horses

"Horses? I don't ride anything I can't put gas into."

Fonzie,
Happy Days

❖

Wilbur Post: "What's new, Ed?"
Mr. Ed: "What can be new with a horse? Just standin' around—eatin', sleepin', and swattin' flies."
Wilbur: "Don't you sometimes wish you were a human being?"
Mr. Ed: "Never. How can you beat eatin', sleepin', and swattin' flies?"
Wilbur: "Beats working, worrying, and paying taxes."
Mr. Ed: "Naturally."

Mr. Ed

Identity

"I am not a number. I am a person."

Number 6,
The Prisoner

❖

Maddie Hayes: "You are exactly the same person as when I walked in here seven months ago."
David Addison: "No wonder these clothes still fit."

Moonlighting

❖

"This is the real me, the new me, the free me that I used to be before I became the old me."

Jerry Robinson,
The Bob Newhart Show

If Brains Was Lard...

"If brains was lard, Jethro couldn't grease a pan."

Jed Clampett,
The Beverly Hillbillies

❖

Dr. Frasier Crane: "I was hoping for some insight."
Diane Chambers: "What insight could you possibly hope to gain from a man whose I.Q. wouldn't make a respectable earthquake?"

Cheers

❖

Lt. Quint: "So I'm 'stupid,' huh? You're going to be sorry for that."
Jake Axminster: "Lieutenant, I was always sorry that you were stupid."

The City of Angels

❖

"When God was handing out brains, he mistook you for a cactus."
Shirley Feeney,
Laverne and Shirley

❖

"Yeah, she's beautiful, but you can't find her I.Q. with a flashlight."
Bill Maxwell,
The Greatest American Hero

❖

"The only way you could ever have a high I.Q. is to go up in a blimp."
Uncle Martin,
My Favorite Martian

❖

"Keep on thinkin'. Someday you'll get good at it."
Sonny Crockett,
Miami Vice

❖

"If brains were money, you'd need to take out a loan to buy a cup of coffee."
Diane Chambers,
Cheers

Immortality

"I plan to live forever, or die trying."

Vila Restal,
Blake's 7

❖

"Immortality consists largely of boredom."

Cochrane,
Star Trek

Individuality

"When you're different, everybody watches you real careful."

Circus Woman,
The Incredible Hulk

❖

"It's better to live as your own man than as a fool in someone else's dream."

John Koenig,
Space: 1999

❖

Trapper John McIntyre: "What about individuality?"
Frank: "Well, individuality is fine. As long as we do it together."

M*A*S*H

❖

"I'm not making any deals with you. . . . I am not going to be pushed, filed, indexed, stamped, briefed, debriefed, or numbered. My life is my own."

Number 6,
The Prisoner

Insurance

Alice Hyatt: "My husband didn't believe in insurance."
Mel Sharples: "How come?"
Alice: "It didn't come in a six-pack."

Alice

❖

"Insurance is no substitute for a good alarm system and a twelve-gauge shotgun."

Victor Isbecki,
Cagney & Lacey

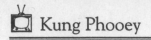
❖

"High insurance rates are what really killed the dinosaurs."

Announcer,
Late Night with David Letterman

❖

"I can't find anyone who'll cover me. Oh, when Bernice finds out I don't have any insurance, it'll kill her . . . and she's not covered either."

Det. Phil Fish,
Barney Miller

Kung Phooey

"Grasshopper, look beyond the game, as you look beneath the surface of the pool to see its depths."

Master Po,
Kung Fu

"The caterpillar is secure in the womb of the cocoon. And yet—to achieve its destiny—it must cast off its earthbound burden . . . to realize the ethereal beauty of the butterfly."

Master Po,
Kung Fu

❖

Master Po: "What is it I have told you, Grasshopper?"
Caine: "That life is a corridor and death merely a door."

Kung Fu

❖

"He who is open-eyed is open-minded. He who is open-minded is open-hearted. He who is open-hearted is kingly. He who is kingly is godly. He who is godly is useful. He who is useful is infinite. He who is infinite is immune. He who is immune is immortal."

Caine,
Kung Fu

❖

"The blossom below the water knows not sunlight. And men, not knowing, will find me hard to understand."

Caine,
Kung Fu

Latin

"I'm taking Latin in school and I can tell you why the Roman Empire declined and fell—because it takes all day to say anything in Latin! I mean, if your house is on fire or Attila the Hun is at the gate and you've gotta stop and think of tenses, cases, and conjugations before you can call for help, brother, you're dead!"

Dobie Gillis,
The Many Loves of Dobie Gillis

❖

" 'Tempus edax rerum.' Time heals everything. You know who said that? My Latin teacher in barber college."

Floyd the Barber,
The Andy Griffith Show

❖

"Good evening. . . . This evening's lecture has as its text the short story 'De Mortuis,' translated from the Latin. This means 'about the dead.' At the risk of being facetious, I would like to point out that Latin is a 'dead' language. . . . Regretably, the author wrote only his title in Latin and did the story in English. Writers are always compromising to obtain commercial success. I shall leave it to your judgment as to whether or not it would have sounded better in Latin."

Alfred Hitchcock,
Alfred Hitchcock Presents

❖

"While you were learning to be a professional gunman, I was back East learning Latin. Now if you'd like to stand toe-to-toe and conjugate verbs, I'm your man."

Ben Maverick,
Maverick

❖

Gomez Addams: "In hoc signo vinces! Non compos mentis! Spiritus fermenti! Caveat emptor! Sic semper tyrannis!"
Morticia Addams: "And they call Latin a dead language!"

The Addams Family

The Law

"I don't hang anyone—the law does."

Marshal Matt Dillon,
Gunsmoke

❖

"All the laws in the world won't stop one man with a gun."

Det. Lt. Mike Stone,
The Streets of San Francisco

❖

Robin: "Batgirl! What took you so long?"
Batgirl: "You wouldn't believe the traffic, and the lights were all against me. Besides, you wouldn't want me to speed, would you?"
Robin: "Your good driving habits almost cost us our lives!"
Batman: "No, Robin, she's right. Rules are rules."

Batman

Lawyers

"Lawyers—can't live with them . . . can't die without them."

Suspect,
Murder, She Wrote

❖

"It's not enough that all the lawyers are crooks, now all the crooks are becomin' lawyers."

Donegan,
Kaz

❖

"The trouble with lawyers is that they are insufferable word stretchers."

Nero Wolfe,
Nero Wolfe

❖

"What is an attorney but a college graduate who couldn't get into medical school?"

Maj. Charles Emerson Winchester,
M*A*S*H

❖

"Lawyers and tarts are the two oldest professions in the world. And we always aim to please."

Horace Rumpole,
Rumpole of the Bailey

❖

"I tell ya—you take all the gray-suited lawyers, you round 'em up and put them on a boat to Indochina, and you wouldn't have no more problems with the criminal justice system in this country."

Officer Andy Renko,
Hill Street Blues

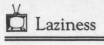
Laziness

"Give a lazy man a job, and he'll find a lazy way to do it."

Roy Rogers,
The Roy Rogers Show

❖

"My father can't understand why I don't like work. What's so hard to understand? Some people don't like artichokes or bow ties or Wyatt Earp. I mean, this is a free country and we all have the right to dislike something. And my choice happens to be work."

Dobie Gillis,
The Many Loves of Dobie Gillis

❖

The Boss: "How about getting to work?"
Kingfish: "Is this an all-day job?"
The Boss: "Put in a full day—eight to five you'll work."
Kingfish: "Eight to five? Well, what's the odds if I don't work?"

Amos 'n' Andy

Leaders and Followers

"I'd rather be a live mouse than a dead boss."

Ed Norton,
The Honeymooners

❖

"I'd rather be a live namby-pamby than a dead executive."

Bud Anderson,
Father Knows Best

❖

"Well, it looks like I've learned another thing about being a leader. If you want to do anything, you've got to do it backwards."

Gomer Pyle,
The Gomer Pyle Show

❖

"I don't have any leadership qualities. . . . In high school I was president of the German Club; nobody would listen to me. If you can't get Germans to follow orders, who will?"

Felix Unger,
The Odd Couple

❖

"Why does everybody have to be a leader? Why can't a guy just be a happy slob?"

Bud Anderson,
Father Knows Best

Learning

"All creatures, the low and the high, are one with nature. If we have the wisdom to learn, all may teach us their virtues."

Caine,
Kung Fu

❖

Howard Cunningham: "You know, there's a lesson to be learned in all of this."
Richie Cunningham: "I figured with all this embarrassment, there had to be a lesson in there somewhere."

Happy Days

❖

"Remember the old slogan—'If you use the method of Socrates you rise above the mediocrities.' "

Wes Carter,
Barnaby Jones

❖

Wally: "Hey, Eddie—how come you're always givin' Beaver the business?"

Eddie: "I'm not givin' him the business. I'm just tryin' to wise him up. I don't want him goin' out in the world and gettin' slaughtered."

Leave It to Beaver

❖

[Singing] "When it comes to learnin', you'd better start at once. There's no use being beautiful if you're a little dunce."

Annette Funicello,
The Mickey Mouse Club

❖

"What a wonderful day we've had. You have learned something, and I have learned something. Too bad we didn't learn it sooner. We could have gone to the movies instead."

Balki Bartokomous,
Perfect Strangers

❖

Boy: "Teach me what you know, Jim."
Reverend Jim Ignatowski: "That would take hours, Terry. Ah, what the heck! We've all got a little Obi Wan Kenobie in us."

Taxi

Legal Fees (fantasy)

Perry Mason: "My fee? Well, what do you think is fair?"
Little Old Lady Client: "Well, I paid you five dollars the first day. It was high, but it was worth it."
Perry: "What do you think now?"
Client: "Well, I want to do the right thing. After all, I could have gone to prison—or even worse. Would twenty-five dollars be all right?"
Perry: "Just exactly the figure I had in mind."
Client: "Well, good. I've got it right here."

Perry Mason

Legal Fees (reality)

"Defending the underdog is fine, but it's usually the upperdog who can pay the big fees."

Alfred Hitchcock,
Alfred Hitchcock Presents

Lies

"That's not a lie, it's a terminological inexactitude."

Alexander Haig,
1983 television news interview

❖

"Nobody lies without a reason."

Adam Flint,
Naked City

❖

Inspector Fenwick: "Let me ask you this, Dudley—how do you fight logic?"
Dudley Do-Right: "Well. . . . "
Fenwick: "By superior deception."

The Bullwinkle Show

❖

"A lie that hurts nobody is not as bad as the truth, which could put me in the slammer."

Kate Foster,
Double Trouble

❖

"Dorothy, a lie is like a snowball. You start out with one little harmless lie, and then you have to tell another one to cover up the first, and then another and another. You know what I mean? And then before long, you've got an entire snowman built out of lies."

Rose,
The Golden Girls

❖

"Virgins don't lie."

Fonzie,
Happy Days

❖

"Always tell the truth. It's the world's best lie."

Uncle Martin,
My Favorite Martian

❖

"A man knows when another man is lying to him. . . . I can't explain how, because maybe I don't know. But this I *do* know—honest men don't deceive each other."

Perry Mason,
Perry Mason

Life

"Life? Don't talk to me about life."

Marvin the Paranoid Android,
The Hitchhiker's Guide to the Galaxy

❖

"The most gratifying reward in life is to feel one is needed."

The Reverend Mother,
The Flying Nun

❖

Wednesday Addams: "It is a black widow spider village."
Gomez Addams: "Amazing, just like a tiny human world."
Wednesday: "Yes, all they do is fight."
Morticia Addams: "Well, that's life."

The Addams Family

❖

"There's more to life than sitting around in the sun in your underwear playing the clarinet."

Lt. Larry Casey,
Baa Baa Black Sheep

❖

Coach Ernie Pantusso: "How's life, Norm?"
Norm Peterson: "It's a dog-eat-dog world, and I'm wearing Milkbone underwear."

Cheers

Life's a Bitch

Beaver: "Gee, there's something wrong with just about everything, isn't there Dad?"
Ward: "Just about, Beav."

Leave It to Beaver

❖

"For a fugitive there are no freeways; all roads are toll roads to be paid in blood and pain."

Narrator,
The Fugitive

❖

"It would be a terrible thing to go through life unhappy and not know how miserable you are."

Frank the gardener,
Father Knows Best

❖

[Explaining why she'd like to win] "I'd like a bird for an old lady of ninety-four. She had one, but it died and she doesn't realize it. She keeps it in a cage, talks to it, and takes it out and kisses its head."

Contestant,
Queen for a Day

❖

"Just remember, things are always darkest just before they go pitch black."

Kelly Robinson,
I Spy

❖

Martin O'Hara: "It's always darkest before the dawn."
Tim O'Hara: "Sure it is! That's usually the hour they shoot people."
My Favorite Martian

❖

"Every silver lining has a cloud."

Kerr Avon,
Blake's 7

❖

"Behind every dark cloud, there's usually rain."

Mike Nesmith,
The Monkees

❖

"Some days you just can't get rid of a bomb."

Batman,
Batman

❖

"God forbid anything should be easy."

Hawkeye Pierce,
*M*A*S*H*

Life in the Fast Lane

"Andy, you gits up at noon, then you rushes to get dressed, then you rushes to the restaurant for breakfast. After you eat, you rushes to the park to take a nap, after you take your nap then you rushes back to eat again; then you rushes home, rushes to get undressed and then you rushes to bed. I tell ya Andy, there's just so much a body can stand."

Kingfish,
Amos 'n' Andy

Life: Is That All There Is?

"Well, isn't life a picnic. . . . I get to be miserable forever . . . I'm just going to have to mope and be unhappy and then one day I'll die."

Stephanie Vanderkellen,
Newhart

[As she folds her son's clothes] "There's got to be more to life than sittin' here watchin' 'Days of Our Lives' and holdin' your Fruit of the Loom."

Mama,
Mama's Family

❖

"Life: loathe it or ignore it, you can't like it."

Marvin the Paranoid Android,
The Hitchhiker's Guide to the Galaxy

❖

Coach Ernie Pantusso: "How's life, Norm?"
Norm Peterson: "Ask somebody who's got one."

Cheers

❖

"It's been the lesson of my life that nothing that sounds that good ever really happens."

Alex Reiger,
Taxi

❖

Hutch: "At least she's alive."
Starsky: "Hey, I've had it up to here with optimistic views of life."

Starsky and Hutch

❖

Life: What Is It?

"Life is just a bag of tricks."

Felix,
The Adventures of Felix the Cat

❖

"Life is not all thorns and singing vultures."

Morticia Addams,
The Addams Family

❖

Ray: "There's more to life than money."
Ty Gardner: "Oh, right. Name me one thing."

Ray: "I'll name ya three: love, friendship, and understanding."
Ty: "Oh, please. Cry me a river, will ya? You forgot about six-foot blondes with big bazookas and teeny-tiny brains."

Stingray

❖

Blanche: "My life is an open book."
Sophia: "Your life is an open blouse."

The Golden Girls

❖

"Life is just a bowl of kumquats."

Contestant,
Jeopardy

❖

"Life is a bowl of green oxtails."

Kip Wilson,
Bosom Buddies

❖

"In life, everything is one of two things—either everything is exactly as it seems or nothing is as it seems. The trick is to know which."

Susan Profit,
Wiseguy

❖

"You know, life's a real bumpy road. What you've got to develop are good shock absorbers."

Uncle Charlie,
My Three Sons

❖

"It's all one big roll of the dice, and nobody loses all the time."

JoAnna Moore,
The Fugitive

❖

"For some people, small beautiful events is what life is all about."

Doctor Who,
Doctor Who

"Life's like a game of marbles. No matter how pretty yours are, the other guy's are prettier."

Gilligan,
Gilligan's Island

❖

"The bus bringeth and the bus taketh away. You know, that's a lot like life."

Floyd Lawson,
The Andy Griffith Show

❖

"Life's a series of bad jokes, and death tops them all."

Dinner guest,
The Saint

Like, Zen

"If closeness is wrong, why are we born with arms? Isn't that sort of Zenlike?"

Mork,
Mork and Mindy

❖

"No river is shallow to a man who can't swim."

Paladin,
Have Gun, Will Travel

❖

"I reek, therefore I am."

Diane Chambers,
Cheers

❖

"I take pills, therefore I am."

Illya Kuryakin,
The Man from U.N.C.L.E.

❖

"It is said that if you move a single pebble on the beach, you set up a different pattern, and everything in the world is changed."

The Control Voice,
The Outer Limits

❖

"Sometimes the best way to hold onto something is to let it go."

Nick Barkley,
The Big Valley

❖

Tortello [after surviving a shoot-out with a professional thief]:
"Yesterday was my birthday. Yesterday was his birthday. Today I killed him. What do you think that means?"
Clemens: "You mean like something cosmic? Some universally fatal conflict, working itself out?"
Tortello: "Yeah, like that."
Clemens: "I think it means next year you'll have a birthday and he won't."

Crime Story

❖

"The butcher with the sharpest knife has the warmest heart."
> Saying in the Village,
> *The Prisoner*

❖

"A lady-in-waiting must learn to wait."
> Gomez Addams,
> *The Addams Family*

❖

"Only a fool fights in a burning house."
> Kang,
> *Star Trek*

❖

"The winter is cold, yet the robin has a song to sing."
> O'Hara,
> *O'Hara*

❖

"Even she, with all the technique I've taught her, cannot teach a noodle to dance."
> Khigh Dhiegh,
> *Noble House* miniseries

❖

Bert: "Do we really exist?"
David Addison: "Bert! Can you feel your underwear?"
Bert: "Yes."
David: "Then we really exist."
> *Moonlighting*

❖

Dobie Gillis: "Oh, hi, good buddy! Whatcha doin'?"
Maynard G. Krebs: "Oh, I was just out pickin' up some tin foil."

Dobie [toThalia]: "Oh. Say, you know, Maynard's got a ball of tin foil this big at home."
Maynard: "Oh, no. Now it's this big."
Dobie: "Really?"
Thalia: "Well, what do you do with it?"
Maynard: "Oh, I pick it up and put it in a ball."
Thalia: "And then what do you do with it?"
Maynard: "I go out and pick up some more."

The Many Loves of Dobie Gillis

❖

"If you do it, then it's done."

Starman,
Starman

❖

Det. Drebin (offering a smoke to a beautiful blonde): "Cigarette?"
Blonde: "Yes, I know."

Police Squad!

❖

"I know they're blue berries, but they might not be blueberries. And while all blueberries are blue berries, not all blue berries are blueberries."

Alex Reiger,
Taxi

❖

Man: "Do you belong here?"
Fonzie: "I belong everywhere."

Happy Days

❖

"We didn't have any room for the 7th floor in this building, so we put it in the building next door. So now it has two 7th floors, which is a very interesting thing to know if you ever go there—which you probably won't, 'cause the building next door is false."

Maxwell Smart,
Get Smart

❖

"Sometimes one must cut off a finger to save a hand."

Master Po,
Kung Fu

❖

"A warped barrel is a fool's frustration."

Maxwell Smart,
Get Smart

❖

"As we say in the sewer, time and tide wait for no man."

Ed Norton,
The Honeymooners

❖

"Time and Ed wait for no man."

Mr. Ed,
Mr. Ed

❖

"One does not thank logic."

Sarek,
Star Trek

❖

"We're all pawns, my dear."

The Admiral,
The Prisoner

❖

Mike: " 'Gilligan's Island' is on every day at three-thirty . . .
  whether I watch it or not!"
Jason: "What's the point?"
Mike: "Dad, it's not on for me. It's just—on!"

Growing Pains

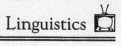
❖

"A day without grapes is like a day without apples."

Kelly Robinson,
I Spy

❖

"Just remember—the eagle may soar but the weasel never gets sucked up into a jet engine."

Rick Simon,
Simon and Simon

❖

"When you don't yell and holler the loudest is when they hear you the most."

Radar O'Reilly,
M*A*S*H

❖

"*That* was the equation! Existence cancels out programming!"

Ruk [a hostile android],
Star Trek

Linguistics

"If you speak three languages, you are trilingual. If you speak two languages, you're bilingual. If you speak one language, you're American."

Sonny Spoon,
Sonny Spoon

❖

The Chief: "Mahanee gonga ghee."
Maxwell Smart: "Gonga ghee? Don't you mean gonga gai?"
Chief: "No. . . . Gonga ghee."
Max: "Really? I always thought it was gai after gonga, except before goo."

Get Smart

❖

"You must always try to keep abreast of other tongues."

Batman,
Batman

The Lone Wolf

Cliff Clavin: "You ever heard of the lone wolf, Carla? The lone wolf, c'est moi. A man by himself, needing no one. I touch no one, no one touches me. I am a rock. I am an island."
Carla Tortelli: "You am a boob."

Cheers

"Living alone has many terrific advantages. You can eat, sleep, go in and out, and burp whenever you want to. It also has its disadvantages—when you lose something you have no one to blame but yourself."

Thomas Magnum,
Magnum, P.I.

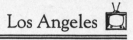
❖

"I never did mind being lonesome by myself. It's being lonesome with somebody that scares me."

Hoss Cartwright,
Bonanza

❖

Vincent: "I've seen your world. There's no place for me in it. I know what I am. Your world is filled with frightened people, and I remind them of what they're most afraid of."
Catherine: "Their own ignorance?"
Vincent: "Their aloneness."

Beauty and the Beast

Los Angeles

"Hey, listen. They call L.A. the city of angels; well let me tell you something—all the angels left this burg about twenty years ago. It's crooked and corrupt and it suits me fine."

Jake Axminster,
The City of Angels

❖

Man: "Well, I've traveled in a great many countries in the foreign service of the government doing personnel work, but Los Angeles is the most wonderful place in the world to live."
Groucho Marx: "Well, I agree, it's a wonderful city, even though I do criticize it occasionally. I'm all for it. And if they'd lower the taxes and get rid of the smog and clean up the traffic mess, I really believe I'd settle here until the next earthquake."

You Bet Your Life

❖

Hobo: "Are we anywhere near Anaheim yet?"
Scrappy: "We must be. My wallet's getting lighter."

The New Adventures of Mighty Mouse

Love

"Love can change the future, if it is deep enough, true enough, and selfless enough. It can prevent a war, prohibit a plague, keep the whole world . . . whole."

> The Control Voice,
> *The Outer Limits*

❖

"We've come to realize that you can be in love without making others want to puke."

> Michael Harris,
> *Newhart*

❖

"There are all kinds of sounds in this wonderful world . . . surely the most beautiful is the sound of love."

> Reverend Mother,
> *The Flying Nun*

❖

"Love stinks."

> Lou Grant,
> *The Mary Tyler Moore Show*

❖

Jack: "You need to know about love, you've come to the right place."
Sam: "Why, have you been in love?"
Jack: "No, but that's good. Anyone who's been in love is all screwed up. I'm still fine."

> *Together We Stand*

❖

"You meet that special person. And you got a special love all saved up for them. That's the marrying kind of love. And that's the very best kind 'cause it comes from way down deep inside your heart."

> Sheriff Andy Taylor,
> *The Andy Griffith Show*

❖

"We all live for love—even lowly scum like you."

Bat-Bat,
The New Adventures of Mighty Mouse

❖

"Son, love and love alone will send a man soaring into the depths."

Pappy Maverick,
Maverick

❖

"Love makes you do funny things. It made me get married."

Buddy Sorrell,
The Dick Van Dyke Show

❖

"I have seen your Earthly love and affection. It is a useless instinct for survival."

Megazor,
Lost in Space

❖

"Love can be as sticky as a vat of molasses, as unpalatable as a hunk of spoiled yeast, and as [out of control] as a six-alarm fire in a bamboo and canvas tent."

Rod Serling,
The Twilight Zone

❖

"Love's the only thing in life you've got to earn. Everything else you can steal."

Pappy Maverick,
Maverick

❖

"There is one power which seems to transcend space and time, life and death. It is a deeply human power which holds us safe and together when all other forces combine to tear us apart. We call it the power of love."

The Control Voice,
The Outer Limits

❖

"Please remember, and don't ever forget: It is better not to have been in love than to never have loved at all."

Dwayne Schneider,
One Day at a Time

❖

"Ah—love—the walks over soft grass, the smiles over candlelight, the arguments over just about everything else. . . . "

Max Headroom,
Max Headroom

❖

"Love means never having to hear the words 'I'm pregnant.'"

Vinnie Barbarino,
Welcome Back, Kotter

❖

"Love is the ultimate trip."

Micky Dolenz,
The Monkees

Magic

"For my grand finale magic act, I will proceed to make my wife disappear—a trick which any husband should appreciate."

Herman Munster,
The Munsters

❖

Martin: "If I took a mixture of potassium nitrate and sugar and ignited it, what do we have?"

Murray: "Simple combustion. Any first-year chem student knows that."

Martin: "Aha! Now, if I took that same mixture and ignited it on a dark stage from my fingertips, then what do we have? [Poof!] Magic."

Murray: "Oh, wow, simple chemistry."

Martin: "Ah, simple, until the mind gets ahold of it."

Riptide

❖

"In any quest for magic, in any search for sorcery, witchery, legerdemain, first check the human heart."

Rod Serling,
The Twilight Zone

❖

"This evening, I shall attempt several feats of legerdemain. One is to make an hour disappear without you realizing it."

Alfred Hitchcock,
Alfred Hitchcock Presents

Mail

George Burns (weighing letter in his hand): "This letter feels kind of heavy. I'd better put another three-cent stamp on it."

Gracie Allen: "What for? It'll only make it heavier."

The George Burns and Gracie Allen Show

❖

"I love getting mail—just the fact that someone licked a stamp just for you is very reassuring."

Thomas Magnum,
Magnum, P.I.

❖

Harry: "You're sending your mother an empty envelope?"

Gracie: "I wanted to cheer her up. You know, no news is good news."

The George Burns and Gracie Allen Show

Makeup

"I haven't worn makeup in years. It takes away that unnatural look that we girls like."

Lily Munster,
The Munsters

❖

Cosmetic Saleslady: "What kind of powder does your mommy use?"
Wednesday Addams: "Baking powder."
Cosmetic Saleslady: "I mean, on her face."
Wednesday: "Baking powder."

The Addams Family

❖

"City women is spoiled rotten. All they think about is smearin' themselves with beauty grease. Fancy smellin' renderin's. Why if you was to hug one of 'em, she'd squirt out of yore arms like a prune pit!"

Granny,
The Beverly Hillbillies

Mama Said

"Like my mama always said, 'It is better to sleep on the beach than be a quitter who raises schnauzers.'"

Aileen Foster,
Double Trouble

❖

"My mom told me never to get into a car with strangers . . . but you're only a little strange."

Carson,
Starsky and Hutch

❖

Arthur Dent: "You know, it's at times like this, when I'm stuck in a Volgon air lock with a man from Betelgeuse, about to die of

asphyxiation in deep space, that I really wish I'd listened to what my mother told me when I was young."
Ford Perfect: "Why? What did she tell you?"
Arthur: "I don't know; I didn't listen."

The Hitchhiker's Guide to the Galaxy

❖

"My mother always said to me 'Son, look the devil in the eye and meet him straight on, you can't wrestle him to the ground unless you've got a hold of him first.' . . . My mother was a babbling fool."

Benson,
Soap

❖

"It's like my mama always says, 'Those who can, do. Those who can't, talk about it so much you want to stuff a sofa cushion up their mouths.' "

Aileen Foster,
Double Trouble

❖

"Mother always told me that when you get into a cab, always check the picture on the back of the seat to make sure it matches the driver. I don't know what good it does, but you do things for your mother."

Laura Petrie,
The Dick Van Dyke Show

❖

"In each of our stories, we try to teach a little lesson or point a little moral—things like Mother taught: 'Walk softly and carry a big stick'; 'Strike first, ask questions after'—that sort of thing."

Alfred Hitchcock,
Alfred Hitchcock Presents

❖

"My mother always used to say: 'The older you get, the better you get—unless you're a banana.' "

Rose,
The Golden Girls

Marriage: Advice to Newlyweds

"A man's home is his castle, and in that castle you're the king . . . Tomorrow afternoon when Agnes says, 'I do,' that is the last decision you allow her to make."

Ralph Kramden [to his brother-in-law-to-be],
The Honeymooners

❖

"Just be considerate, accept each other for what you are, and don't point out the fact that the hair he's losing on his head is now growing out of his nose—and his ears."

Peg Bundy,
Married...with Children

❖

"I want to tell you the truth about marriage, son: it's impossible. As impossible as making it into the big leagues. As impossible as making a million dollars. As impossible as doing the right things for your kids so that when they grow up, they love you as much as you love them. And the damn catch is that the only thing that keeps us from being a nation of empty suits is that every now and then we go for the impossible. And today, son, you're going to go for the impossible."

John Lucey,
Dear John

Marriage: To Wed or Not to Wed?

"You and I are good friends. I'd hate for marriage to get between us."

Flo Castleberry,
Alice

❖

"Look, boys, Joan Hogan is a beautiful, highly intelligent and sophisticated girl. We're too much alike to get married."

Sgt. Bilko,
The Phil Silvers Show

❖

"I don't want to be married. I don't know—it sounds crazy, but in my mind, it's all connected. You get married, you have kids, you grow old, then you die. Somehow, it seems to me, if you didn't get married, you wouldn't die."

John Burns,
Taxi

❖

"Son, stay clear of weddings because one of them is liable to be your own."

Pappy Maverick,
Maverick

Maxwell Smart: "You know, Ninety-nine, if we could get out of this trap I'd marry you."
Agent 99: "You would?"
Max: "Of course I would."
99: "Now that you mention it, Max, there is a way out."
Max: "There is?"
99: "What about the old double-door deception trick! It just might work!"
Max: "Of course! The old double-door deception trick! It just might work!"
99: "If it does we'll get out of here alive and then we can be married. [Max freezes] Max! Don't you want to get out of here alive?"
Max: "I'm thinking."

Get Smart

❖

Della Street: "What is it that makes a man wait all those years to get married?"
Perry Mason: "You've been my legal secretary long enough to know that's a leading question."

Perry Mason

❖

Claire Huxtable: "If I died, would you marry again?"
Cliff Huxtable: "We'll talk about it when it happens."

The Cosby Show

❖

Mrs. Davis: "Give Mr. Boynton a subtle hint or two."
Miss Brooks: "Like what, for instance?"
Mrs. Davis: "Tell him you're sick and tired of being single."
Miss Brooks: "Oh, that's fine—or maybe I could dump a bowl of rice over his head and whistle the wedding march."

Our Miss Brooks

Marriage: Taking the Plunge

"Well, well, well. . . . So you're gonna get married, ha, ha, ha. Welcome to the ranks of the living dead."

Kingfish,
Amos 'n' Andy

❖

"Marriage is a serious step. . . . even for a horse."

Wilbur Post,
Mr. Ed

❖

"It's time you got married and realized that happiness isn't the only thing in life."

Carolyn Muir,
The Ghost and Mrs. Muir

❖

Dwayne Schneider: "I'm gonna ask Miss Wroblicki to tie the knot."
Anne Romano: "You're gonna ask her to marry you?"
Schneider: "I ain't talkin' about a vasectomy."

One Day at a Time

Marriage: The Wedding

"You've got to practice feeding me the cake so I get just enough icing on the tip of my cute little nose to make it seem like I'm a good sport."

Stephanie Vanderkellen,
Newhart

❖

Murray Greshler: "Felix, why isn't Gloria wearing white?"
Felix Unger: "Murray, Gloria is the mother of two children."
Murray: "Oh, I suppose it is hard to keep things white with children around."

The Odd Couple

❖

"Here comes the bride, all dressed in yella;
She'd be in white, but she had another fella."

Louie Wilson,
Chico and the Man

Marriage: Wedded Bliss

Imogene Coca: "I just can't understand it. I expected their marriage to go on forever. They had so much in common, you know."
Sid Caesar: "That's right. The same interests. They like the same things."
Coca: "He liked baseball."
Caesar: "And so did she."
Coca: "He liked to collect stamps."

Caesar: "And so did she."
Coca: "He liked to go out with the boys at night and drink and play poker and smoke cigars."
Caesar: "And so did she."

Your Show of Shows

❖

Groucho Marx: "How long have you been married?"
Woman: "Three wonderful years."
Groucho: "Never mind the wonderful years. How many miserable years have you had?"

You Bet Your Life

❖

"We weren't married. We were temporarily insane in front of a judge."

Michael,
A Fine Romance

❖

Husband [about wife]: "Lousy, sloppy drunk—"
Sgt. Joe Friday: "Don't knock her—she's had a good reason to drink."
Husband: "And what's that?"
Friday: "She was married to you."

Dragnet

❖

"Since the day I married you thirteen years ago, there's *never* been a man in my life!"

Blanche Morton,
The George Burns and Gracie Allen Show

❖

Gladys Kravitz [the nosy neighbor, after seeing Samantha transform herself into an animal]: "I bet she has some strange disease and we can catch it. You want to wake up with something strange?"
Abner Kravitz [her husband]: "I've been doing that for twenty years. Why change now?"

Bewitched

❖

Archie Bunker: "After twenty-seven years of marriage you would call me dumb?"
Edith Bunker: "I'm sorry Archie, I shouldn't have waited so long."

All in the Family

Alice Kramden: "Boy, you men kill me. You're all alike. You push us around; you want us to bow and scrape at your feet; all you do is yell and scream and give us orders. You men think you own the world."
Ralph Kramden: "Yeah, but you women get revenge—you marry us."

The Honeymooners

❖

"If you expect perpetual minute-to-minute romance from a marriage, you're in trouble."

Steve Douglas,
My Three Sons

❖

"You know, universal military training is a great idea. It prepares a kid for marriage."

George Burns,
The George Burns and Gracie Allen Show

❖

"Tie yourself up with some chick and pretty soon she's gonna be
making you eat with a knife and fork."

Juan Epstein,
Welcome Back, Kotter

❖

Maggie: "You told me that total honesty is essential to a happy
   marriage."
Jason: "I said that *after* we were married?"

Growing Pains

❖

Julie: "Roseanne, listen to this: 'Utah Housewife Stabs Husband 37
   Times.'"
Roseanne: "I admire her restraint."

Roseanne

❖

[Wearing a prisoner's ball and chain] "I've consented to stand here
like a watch fob in order to dramatize one of our oldest
institutions—an institution which seeks to rehabilitate men by
keeping them shut up for years . . . marriage."

Alfred Hitchcock,
Alfred Hitchcock Presents

❖

Lucy Ricardo: "Mmmm. We have had fun, haven't we, honey?"
Ricky Ricardo: "Yessir. These fifteen years have been the best years
   of my life. [Sees Lucy is upset.] What's the matter?"
Lucy: "We've only been married thirteen years."
Ricky: "Oh. Well. . . . I mean . . . it *seems* like fifteen."
Lucy: "What!"
Ricky: "No . . . uh . . . uh . . . uh . . . what I mean is, it doesn't . . . uh
   . . . seem possible . . . that all that fun could have been crammed
   into only thirteen years."
Lucy: "Well, you certainly wormed out of that one."

I Love Lucy

❖

"I married you for better or worse—when's it gonna start getting better?"

> Helen Roper,
> *Three's Company*

❖

Commissioner Gordon: "Have you ever been married?"
Alfred the Butler: "Well . . . no."
Gordon: "Alfred, at the risk of sounding pompous, experience with
women and experience with *wives* are two vastly different things."
Police Chief O'Hara: "Amen."

> *Batman*

❖

B.J. Hunnicut: "I'm happily married."
Hawkeye Pierce: "Oh yeah? I thought that was a contradiction in
terms."

> *M*A*S*H*

❖

"That shows how long we've been married. Now you kiss me to calm me down."

> Joan Davis,
> *I Married Joan*

❖

Lucy Ricardo [at a party]: "See what I mean? Women in one room,
men in the other."
Ethel Mertz: "Well?"
Lucy: "What do you mean, 'Well?' Why does it have to be that way?
Why aren't we all in here talking together? Give me one good
reason."
Ethel: "We're married."

> *I Love Lucy*

❖

"My wife. . . . I think I'll keep her."

Geritol Commercial

❖

"Why can't somebody invent something for us to marry besides women?"

Fred Flintstone,
The Flintstones

Masculinity

"Masculinity often manifests itself in the way a person talks. The number of words per sentence is in direct inverse proportion to the amount of manliness affected in any given response."

Nick Ryder,
Riptide

Ward Cleaver: "You know, Wally, shaving is just one of the outward signs of being a man. It's more important to try to be a man inside first."
Wally Cleaver: "Yeah sure, Dad."

Leave It to Beaver

❖

Thomas Magnum: "The sleeves are going to be too short."
Woman: "Real men roll up their sleeves."

Magnum, P.I

❖

Herbert: "This is work for men."
Dr. Who: "What I'm about to do is very dangerous. There's nothing particularly masculine about throwing your life away."

Dr. Who

❖

"He's not man enough to pull on stretch socks."

Endora,
Bewitched

Material Possessions

"Just keep in mind that material possessions are just excess baggage in the journey of life."

Reverend Jim Ignatowski,
Taxi

❖

Ricky Ricardo: "There you go again, wanting something that you haven't got."
Lucy Ricardo: "I do not. I just want to see what I haven't got that I don't want."

I Love Lucy

❖

"After a time, you may find that having is not so pleasing a thing, after all, as wanting. It is not logical, but it is often true."

Spock,
Star Trek

Men

"Men are nothing but lazy lumps of drunken flesh. They crowd you in bed, get you all worked up, and then before you can say 'Is that all there is?' that's all there is."

Mrs. Gravas (Latka's Mother),
Taxi

❖

"Men are such idiots and I married their king."

Peg Bundy,
Married...With Children

❖

"Let me give you a little insight into the male psychosis, okay? A male is not going to show his true color unless the female intimates a certain curiosity. A man needs encouragement, he needs reassurance—a toss of the head, a wink of the eye, a flash of the thigh. It's the law of nature."

Dwayne Schneider,
One Day at a Time

Mental Health

"Ryder's Law: People generally get out of the way of crazies."

Nick Ryder,
Riptide

❖

"It's bad luck to take advice from insane people."

Herb Tarlek,
WKRP in Cincinnati

❖

"I don't care if you're psychotic—just don't *whine* about it.

Det. Ron Harris,
Barney Miller

❖

Bob Hartley: "Howard, what do you do when you're upset?"
Howard Borden: "Well, I've got a method—it always works. I go into a dark room, open up all the windows, take off all my clothes, and eat something cold. No, wait a minute, I do that when I'm overheated. When I have a problem I just go to pieces."

The Bob Newhart Show

❖

"We have nothing to fear but sanity itself."

Mork,
Mork and Mindy

❖

"I'm very organized. I have this very elaborate schedule. Sure sign of mental health, huh?"

Elaine Nardo,
Taxi

❖

[Throwing open the window of their apartment and sticking her head out] "Listen, America! My husband is a NUT!"

Lucille Toody,
Car 54, Where Are You?

❖

"You're obviously suffering from delusions of adequacy."

Alexis Carrington,
Dynasty

❖

"The key to handling a disturbed mind is a caring hand, not an iron fist."

Psychiatrist,
Night Court

❖

"Crazy people alphabetize the spice rack."

Allie Lowell,
Kate and Allie

❖

Mrs. Bakerman [to her psychiatrist]: "Dr. Hartley, if you're looking
for a new member of our group, I know a nice schizophrenic."
Mr. Peterson: "Or how about a manic-depressive? At least you know
they'll be fun half the time."

The Bob Newhart Show

❖

"Some day your Mr. Right will come along. And when he does, he's
gonna be wearing a white coat and a butterfly net."

Louie DePalma,
Taxi

The Mind

"The curious mind cannot be chained. It is a free mind, endlessly
searching for the greater freedom that must eventually make every
living being joyfully complete within himself, therefore at peace with
himself and his neighbors."

The Control Voice,
The Outer Limits

❖

Fred Beamer: "The mind is a wonderful tool, Jim."
Jim Rockford: "How would you know?"

The Rockford Files

❖

Crystal: "Do you realize that most people use two percent of their
mind's potential?"
Roseanne: "That much, huh?"

Roseanne

❖

"Why can't your mind be as open as your mouth always is?"

Uncle Martin,
My Favorite Martian

Mom

"You can can fool some of the people all of the time, and all of the people some of the time, but *you can't fool Mom!*"

Captain Penny,
WEWS *TV, Cleveland*

❖

Morticia Addams: "Now Pugsley darling, who could be closer than a boy and his mother?"
Puggsley Addams: "A boy and his octopus?"
Morticia [smiling]: "Hmmm . . . Perhaps."

The Addams Family

❖

"I wish I was Donna Reed—she'd have something wonderful to say. . . . Or Shirley Jones—she'd have something wonderful to say, too, and maybe even some fresh-baked cookies. . . . Or Loretta Young; of course, she wouldn't have anything wonderful to say, but she *would* make a stunning entrance."

Jessica Tate,
Soap

❖

"What *Mother* knows best is how to prove she's right."

Endora,
Bewitched

❖

"It is not easy being a mother. If it were easy, fathers would do it."

Dorothy,
The Golden Girls

❖

"I guess being a mother sometimes interferes with logic."

June Cleaver,
Leave It to Beaver

❖

"You haven't had a meaningful relationship with a woman since your mother quit breastfeeding you."

Henry Goldblume,
Hill Street Blues

❖

"I know how to do anything—I'm a mom."

Roseanne,
Roseanne

❖

Allen Funt: "If you were a mommy would you spank your baby?"
Kid: "No! Well, not when it's *real* little . . . not until pretty near at least . . . uh . . . one year old . . . 'cause that's when it kinda learns to know a little better . . . then POW! Yeah."

Candid Camera

Money

Marilyn: "Is there anything you won't do for money?"
Rockford: "Well, there's two things. I won't kill for it and I won't marry for it. Other than that, I'm open to about anything."

The Rockford Files

❖

"Money speaks all languages."

J.R. Ewing,
Dallas

❖

"There's only one thing more important than money, and that's more money."

Pappy Maverick,
Maverick

❖

"Money seems to have a rubberlike quality because you can bounce a check or stretch a dollar."

Mork,
Mork and Mindy

❖

"Let that be a lesson to you. Never do anything for money. Only do those things you enjoy doing."

Illya Kuryakin,
The Man from U.N.C.L.E.

❖

"I'm mad that money counts for everything in this world—and that I don't have any."

Alex Reiger,
Taxi

❖

"Actually, I have no regard for money. Aside from its purchasing power, it's completely useless as far as I'm concerned."

Alfred Hitchcock,
Alfred Hitchcock Presents

❖

"Where there's man, there's money."

Woman,
Gunsmoke

❖

"Money is something you never spend, you just make more of it."
Thurston Howell III,
Gilligan's Island

Money Management

Kingfish: "What do you mean, you can't cash this check? I got an account here, now gimme one good reason!"
Bank Teller: "We can't cash it because of insufficient funds."
Kingfish: "What do you mean, insufficient funds? They got a sign out there on your front door in gold letters sayin' that you got 38 million dollars surplus."
Teller: "Mr. Stevens, *your* balance is $2.96."

Amos 'n' Andy

❖

A.J. Simon: "Didn't you make the payments on the truck?
Rick Simon: "Some of them."
A.J.: "The point is to make *all* of them. What do you do with your paychecks, origami?"

Simon and Simon

❖

Ralph Kramden: "I ain't cheap. There's a big difference between bein' cheap and bein' thrifty. I have to look after my money, Alice. It don't grow on trees for me. I got to work for it. I didn't inherit it from no rich father. I wasn't born with no silver spoon in my mouth, you know."
Alice Kramden: "No, you were born with a fork in your mouth and you've been eating ever since!"

The Honeymooners

❖

Sampson: "You're looking at the only American soldier who took a Japanese prisoner and tried to hold him for ransom."
Sgt. Ernie Bilko: "That's a lie. I was just trying to show the general staff how we could run the war at a profit."

The Phil Silvers Show

❖

Dick Loudon: "Half the fun of having money is spending it on things you don't need."
George Utley: "What's the other half?"

Newhart

❖

Ralph Kramden: "Before I let you go to work, I'd rather see you starve. We'll just have to live on our savings."
Alice Kramden: "That'll carry us through the night, but what will we do in the morning?"

The Honeymooners

Morning

"Now I know why they shoot people at sunrise—who wants to live at six a.m.?"

**Hawkeye Pierce,
M*A*S*H**

❖

"Nothing ever makes sense first thing in the morning."

**Jack Dane,
*Daktari***

Music

"Music begins where words leave off."

**Saying in the Village,
*The Prisoner***

❖

"Got time to breathe, you got time for music."

Briscoe Darling,
The Andy Griffith Show

❖

"I know George is a great music lover, because a poet once said that every man kills the thing he loves, and I've heard what George does to a song."

Harry Von Zell,
The George Burns and Gracie Allen Show

❖

"It's a strange quirk, but I hardly ever sing along with people who tie me up."

Mork,
Mork and Mindy

❖

Laura Holt: "Dead men don't sing."
Remington Steele: "Thank God for that."

Remington Steele

❖

"These are bagpipes. I understand the inventor of the bagpipes was inspired when he saw a man carrying an indignant, asthmatic pig under his arm. Unfortunately, the man-made sound never equalled the purity of the sound achieved by the pig."

Alfred Hitchcock,
Alfred Hitchcock Presents

Names

Wilbur Post: "Ed? What kind of a name is 'Ed' for a horse?"
Mr. Ed: "What kind of a name is 'Wilbur' for a man?"

Mr. Ed

❖

"Well, now that you're here, we may as well get to know each other. My name is Peabody. I suppose you know yours."

Mr. Peabody,
The Bullwinkle Show

Narcissism: The I's Have It

Ted Baxter: "It's a great experience to appear before a federal grand jury. I told them I was the best newsman in the country."
Murray Slaughter: "You didn't."
Ted: "I had to. I was under oath."

The Mary Tyler Moore Show

❖

"He who blows his own horn only ends up with a fat lip."

Herman Munster,
The Munsters

❖

"I hate to blow my own horn, but 'Beep Beep.'"

Alex Keaton,
Family Ties

❖

"Humble, that's me . . . Mr. Modesty. When it comes to humility, I'm the greatest."

Bullwinkle,
The Bullwinkle Show

❖

Agent 99 [expressing her love]: "Oh Max, you're so brave, so
   dedicated, so wonderful."
Maxwell Smart: "I understand, Ninety-nine. I feel the same way."
99: "Oh, Max, then say it, say it."
Maxwell: "I'm brave and dedicated and wonderful."

Get Smart

❖

Blanche: "Italian men are just the sexiest, most romantic, most
   gorgeous men in the world; and of course, they just worship me
   'cause I'm blond and feminine, and young with a great body."
Dorothy: "What mirror do you use?"

The Golden Girls

❖

"Don't start comparing yourself with me. It will only make you crazy."
Det. Ron Harris,
Barney Miller

Nature

"It's not for mortals like us to tamper with nature."

Batman,
Batman

❖

Thomas Magnum: "Once nature starts its course, you can't stop it."
Jonathan Higgins: "You can if you're British!"

Magnum, P.I.

❖

"It's hard to be natural when you're wearing a toupee, contact lenses,
and four-inch lifts."

Mr. Carlin,
The Bob Newhart Show

❖

"Daisies will tell. You just have to torture them a little."

Laugh-In

❖

"As no two elements of nature are in conflict, so . . . when we perceive the ways of nature, we remove conflict within ourselves and discover a harmony of body and mind in accord with the flow of the universe."

Caine,
Kung Fu

❖

"Never wear polyester underwear if you're going to be hit by lightning."

Roz,
Night Court

The Nature of Man

"Some of us change, some of us mutate."

Joyce Davenport,
Hill Street Blues

❖

"I'm only human, Meathead . . . and to be human is to be violent."
Archie Bunker,
All in the Family

❖

Mr. Spock: "A feeling is not much to go on."
Captain Kirk: "Sometimes a feeling, Mr. Spock, is all we humans have to go on."

Star Trek

❖

"We seem to have a compulsion these days to bury time capsules in order to give those people living in the next century or so some idea of what we are like. I have prepared one of my own. In it, I have placed some rather large samples of dynamite, gunpowder, and nitroglycerin. My time capsule is set to go off in the year 3000. It will show them what we are really like."

Alfred Hitchcock,
Alfred Hitchcock Presents

❖

"Human beings are endlessly creative. They're always looking for new ways to do things, new ideas. That is what makes you so special and unique."

Starman,
Starman

❖

"It took a war to make me realize that most people are degenerate."

Gen. Wainwright Purdy III,
M*A*S*H

❖

"We're all animals, ma'am, akin to the beasts of the field. The only difference is that man knows he's going to die."

Cowboy,
The Big Valley

❖

"I think man is the most interesting insect, don't you?"

Marvin Martian,
The Bugs Bunny Show

❖

"The only good human is a dead human."

General Urco,
The Planet of the Apes

❖

"Man produces little that is lasting—truly lasting. It's understandable. Fear, conformity, immorality; these are heavy burdens. Great drainers of creative energy. And when we are drained of creative energy we do not create. We procreate; we do not create."

Gwyllm Griffiths,
The Outer Limits

❖

"Strange, isn't it, how people manage to ignore those things that they can't understand."

McGee,
The Incredible Hulk

❖

"There is a growing tendency to think of Man as a rational being, which is absurd. There is simply no evidence of any intelligence on the earth."

Marvin Martian,
The Bugs Bunny Show

❖

Kristin: "Familiarity breeds contempt, is that what you're saying?"
J.R.: "Oh, I wouldn't say contempt exactly. . . . But it *does* take some of the bloom off the rose, don't you think?"

Dallas

❖

"There's so much good in the worst of us, and so many of the worst of us get the best of us, that the rest of us aren't even worth talking about."

Gracie Allen,
The George Burns and Gracie Allen Show

❖

Mr. Spock: "May I point out that I had an opportunity to observe your counterparts . . . quite closely. They were brutal, savage, unprincipled, uncivilized, treacherous—in every way, splendid

examples of Homo Sapiens. The very flower of humanity. I found them quite refreshing."
Captain Kirk [to Dr. McCoy]: "I'm not sure, but I think we've been insulted."

Star Trek

❖

"Everyone's a character—some of us just haven't met the right writer yet."

Dash Goff,
Designing Women

Never Say Never

"Never send a man to do a horse's job."

Mr. Ed,
Mr. Ed

❖

"Never clarify tomorrow what you can obscure today."

Laugh-In

❖

"Never trust a wolf's tameness, a horse's health, or an enemy's smile."
Israel Boone,
Daniel Boone

❖

"Never be ashamed of solving the mystery of mass murder."
Mary Hartman,
Mary Hartman, Mary Hartman

❖

"Never ever pick a fight,
'Cause it never ever proves who's right."

The Howdy Doody Show

New York City

Aunt Margo: "How was New York today, Allison?"
Allison Foster: "Ah, I finally found something here that reminds me of Iowa—the buses. They're like cattle cars. You could die in one and nobody would know, or care. I don't know why I bother with clean underwear."

Double Trouble

❖

"Interesting survey in the current *Journal of Abnormal Psychology*. New York City has a higher percentage of people you shouldn't make any sudden moves around than any other city in the world."

David Letterman,
Late Night with David Letterman

❖

"Barbecue in New York? You'd have to keep vacuuming the meat."

Joe Gerard,
Rhoda

❖

"Every year when it's Chinese New Year here in New York, there are fireworks going off at all hours. New York mothers calm their frightened children by telling them it's just gunfire."

David Letterman,
Late Night with David Letterman

❖

Barney Miller: "I'm sure getting robbed at knifepoint and spending half the night up here wasn't exactly what you had in mind when you decided to visit New York."
Lady: "Well, it was better than seeing *Annie*."

Barney Miller

❖

"Tip to out-of-town visitors: If you buy something here in New York and want to have it shipped home, be suspicious if the clerk tells you they don't need your name and address."

David Letterman,
Late Night with David Letterman

❖

Victim: "You know, I watched all those 'I Love New York' commercials back in Youngstown—with all the Broadway actors singing and dancing—they're so exciting and colorful. But they never mention the people with knives."
Det. Ron Harris: "Well, they only have a minute."

Barney Miller

The News

[Looking at a newspaper] "Sex and Crime—America's favorite breakfast diet."

Gomez Addams,
The Addams Family

❖

"When a boy tells a lie, it can cause trouble; but when a newspaper tells a lie, it can cause more than trouble. People are liable to find the newspaper a hundred years from now and believe it."

Wyatt Earp,
The Life and Legend of Wyatt Earp

Nice Girls

Sue Ann Nivens: "Mary, what do you think turns on a man?"
Mary Richards (exasperated): "Sue Ann, I haven't the slightest idea."
Sue Ann: "I know that, dear. I was just trying to make your day."

The Mary Tyler Moore Show

❖

Jack Tripper: "She's pure and wholesome and virtuous. Whatever happened to girls like that?"
Janet Wood: "They all go out with guys like you."

Three's Company

❖

Felix Unger: "I like my women quiet, ladylike, attractive, and refined."
Oscar Madison: "What for?"

The Odd Couple

Nonviolence

"Look, Colonel, I'll fix their wounds, bind their wounds, clean their wounds, operate on their wounds, but I will *not* inflict their wounds."

**Hawkeye Pierce,
M*A*S*H**

"Now, now, Eddie, sensitive intelligent creatures such as we do not stomp one another."

**Herman Munster,
The Munsters**

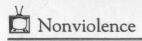
❖

"Don't be a noble fighter, 'cause kindness is righter."

Popeye,
The Popeye Cartoon Show

❖

Student: "What is the best way to deal with force?"
Teacher: "As we prize peace and quiet above victory, there is a simple and preferred method—run away."

Kung Fu

Captain Kirk: "Yes, gentlemen, you have a real war on your hands. You can either wage it, with real weapons, or you might consider an alternative. Put an end to it—make peace."
Council Leader: "There can be no peace. Don't you see, we've admitted it to ourselves. We're a killer species. It's instinctive. It's the same with you. . . . "
Kirk: "All right! It's instinctive. . . . But the instinct can be fought. We're human beings with the blood of a million savage years on our hands but we can stop it! We can admit that we're killers, but we're not going to kill today. That's all it takes—knowing that you're not going to kill . . . TODAY!"

Star Trek

❖

"Holler, but don't hit."

Mr. Ed,
Mr. Ed

Nostalgia

Orson: "Mork, you seem to like the fifties."
Mork: "Yes, sir. It's a wonderful, naive, and romantic time. . . . But you know, they all seem to block out one thing: Senator McCarthy."
Orson: "Ah, yes—those were sad days."
Mork: "I guess that's why it's so romantic—they never remember the sad things."

Happy Days

Nuclear War

"A man learns a great deal from sitting on top of an armed nuclear bomb for twenty-four hours."

Admiral Nelson,
Voyage to the Bottom of the Sea

❖

Alex Keaton: " 'Deterrent force,' Jen. It means that the more weapons that both sides have the less chance that either side will have to use them."
Jennifer Keaton: "Why can't both sides just have no bombs?"
Alex: "It's too late—we already paid for them."

Family Ties

❖

Agent 99: "Oh, Max, what a terrible weapon of destruction."
Maxwell Smart: "Yes. You know, China, Russia, and France should outlaw all nuclear weapons. We should insist upon it."

99: "What if they won't, Max?"
Smart: "Then we may have to blast them. That's the only way to
    keep peace in the world."

Get Smart

❖

"These kind people are working on a missile which in time of trouble
is going to solve all our problems by blowing up the world."

Herman Munster,
The Munsters

Nudity

"Don't argue in front of your children. It bruises their psyches. They
may never be able to skinny-dip in the nude."

Dwayne Schneider,
One Day at a Time

❖

"Nudity? Nudity? What's wrong with nudity. Beneath our clothes we
all stand naked."

Chico Rodriguez,
Chico and the Man

Opportunity

"Opportunity can't knock unless it's on your doorstep."
Wall Street Journal commercial

❖

"How do you like my luck? Every time opportunity knocks I ain't got
enough money to open the door."

Sgt. Ernie Bilko,
The Phil Silvers Show

Paranoia

"When everyone is out to get you, paranoia is only good thinking."
Johnny Fever,
WKRP in Cincinnati

Parents

"My parents don't understand me. Of course, a lot of the time, *I* don't understand me. But they're supposed to be smarter than I am."
Dobie Gillis,
The Many Loves of Dobie Gillis

"Some parents get better children than they deserve."

Perry Mason,
Perry Mason

❖

Jennifer Keaton: "I hate it when Mom and Dad fight—it makes me nervous."
Mallory Keaton: "Me too. It's terrible."
Alex Keaton: "These fights are natural. It happens once every few years—it's very cleansing. Let me tell you something. At times like this when they fight, they're off balance—they need support. And they're going to be looking to us, their children, for validation and love. They're very vulnerable. It's a perfect time to hit them up for gifts."

Family Ties

❖

"There must be some way of getting into the world without going through parents."

Dobie Gillis,
The Many Loves of Dobie Gillis

❖

"I don't care what kind of trouble you may get into in life—you don't ever need to be afraid to come to your parents and tell them."

Ward Cleaver,
Leave It to Beaver

❖

Rob Petrie: "Mel, how could you make a mistake like that?"
Buddy Sorrell: "Easy, it's heredity. Look at the mistake his parents made."

The Dick Van Dyke Show

❖

"When your child is in trouble, you defend him without question, without reservation."

Victoria Barkley,
The Big Valley

❖

Claire Huxtable [exasperated]: "Why do we have five children?"
Cliff Huxtable: "Because we did not want to have six."

The Cosby Show

❖

"I think our parents got together in 1946 and said, 'Let's have lots of kids and give them everything they want, so that they can grow up and be totally messed up and unable to cope with life.'"

Hope Steadman,
thirtysomething

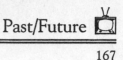
❖

"Parents are like cars . . . built-in obsolescence.

Harvey Lacey,
Cagney and Lacey

Past / Future

Caine: "You once told me the present is rooted in the past."
Master Po: "And it is through those roots we draw our nourishment
  and strength."
Caine: "Do not, then, the roots also form the future?"
Master Po: "Uprooted, can the plant flourish and flower? . . .
  Without the flower, can the hummingbird sip the sweet nectar of
  its bloom and, thus, fulfill the ordained cycle of the universe?"
Caine: "Then my future lies in my past."

Kung Fu

❖

"Some people carry their past. Some people hide from it. Sometimes
you can't do either."

Ray,
Stingray

❖

"A man is the sum of his memories."

Doctor Who,
Doctor Who

❖

"It's fine to turn over a new leaf,
but there's always somebody trying
to snoop through the old pages."
Pappy Maverick,
Maverick

Peace

"It's sad that with all man's genius he's never been able to invent a lasting peace."

Henry Abington,
The Young Rebels

❖

"Seek always peace. . . . We are all linked by our souls, and if one is endangered so are all."

Caine,
Kung Fu

People

"There's no map, there's no master plan, there's just people."

Ray,
Stingray

❖

Allen Funt: "Why are people born?"
Kid: "Well, the whole world should not be covered with nothing."

Candid Camera

❖

"There are going to be people who will take advantage of you, but there are other people, kind and loving people. They'll give you the tools to live a life of courage, and pride and joy."

Starman,
Starman

❖

"People who don't like dragons—who knows *what* they'll do!"

Morticia Addams,
The Addams Family

Philosophy of Life

"One man's ceiling is another man's floor."

Mork,
Mork and Mindy

❖

Art Linkletter: "Do you have a philosophy of life?"
Kid: "Don't goof off. Don't mess around. Don't flub up."

Art Linkletter's House Party

❖

"Sneaky ways are always the best ways."

Julie McCoy,
The Love Boat

❖

"You must either be a hammer or an anvil."

Number 6,
The Prisoner

❖

Narrator: Anyone who went past the third grade surely must remember the thinkings of the great thinker, Hypotenuse. It was he
who said..."
Hypotenuse: "Tibi fumus obsideo septem doro."
Narrator: "... Which roughly translated means 'everybody can do
something.' How very true that is. Take Otis Gumm of Owl's Eye,
Nebraska, for example. He can put six flashlights in his mouth at
one time. And let us not forget Adler Suggins. Mr. Suggins went
over Niagara Falls sitting on a large bagel. No one had ever done
that before. Adler Suggins only did it once."

The Bullwinkle Show

❖

Anne Romano: "You can't hide your head in the sand."
Julie Cooper: "Unless you have feathers on your butt."

One Day at a Time

❖

"My dad once gave me a few words of wisdom which I've always tried to live by. He said, 'Son, never throw a punch at a redwood.' "

Thomas Magnum,
Magnum P.I.

❖

"Sometimes the easy road ain't the right one."

Mathew Hancock,
The Oregon Trail

❖

"My philosophy of life, Mildred, is that nothing in life is worth doing unless it can be accomplished with a short cut."

Remington Steele,
Remington Steele

❖

"I'm a lucky guy—I mean, life has been good to me. I've got a good job, good health, a good wife, and a fantastic barber."

Ted Baxter,
The Mary Tyler Moore Show

Playboy Magazine

"If Hugh Hefner truly thinks that being publicly spread-eagled is so fantastic, how come we haven't seen his little wahoo with a staple in the middle?"

Julia Sugarbaker,
Designing Women

❖

Jim Rockford: "Sandra, all the men in the world don't subscribe to *Playboy*."
Sandra: "Do you?"
Jim: "Uh, no—I borrow my father's copy when he's through."

The Rockford Files

Poetry

"Flowers wilt and candy's sweet,
But thermal socks will warm your feet."

> Dr. Charley Michaels,
> *House Calls*

❖

"Life is real, life is earnest,
If you're cold, turn up the furnace."

> Herman Munster,
> *The Munsters*

❖

"A little song, a little dance,
A little seltzer down your pants."

> Chuckles the Clown,
> *The Mary Tyler Moore Show*

❖

"Ladies and gents, take my advice,
Pull down your pants, and slide on the ice."

> Dr. Sidney Freedman,
> *M*A*S*H*

❖

"Fair or foul weather,
We must all stick together."

> Underdog,
> *Underdog*

❖

"When the tides of life turn against you,
    And the current upsets your boat,
Don't waste those tears on what might have been,
    Just lay on your back and float."

> Ed Norton,
> *The Honeymooners*

Politics

Bud Abbott: "He's not a Republican. He's not a Democrat. He's a cross between a Republican and a Democrat."
Heckler: "He sure is. He eats like an elephant and thinks like a jackass."

The Abbott and Costello Show

❖

Rocky Rockford: "Them politicians—always making a mess of things."
Jim Rockford: "Yeah, Dad? When was the last time *you* voted?"

The Rockford Files

❖

Ralph: "Everybody knows that a wife has to vote the same way that her husband votes. It's been goin' on for years."
Alice: "Oh, that's absolutely ridiculous, Ralph. A woman votes the way she wants to vote, not the way her husband tells her to."
Ralph: "How come all of a sudden you wanna vote for Harper? I know why you wanna vote for him. . . . Cause he's handsome, that's why. 'Cause he's got a mustache. That's all you women ever vote for—mustaches."

The Honeymooners

❖

"No man has the right, nor will the checks and balances of the universe permit him, to place his fellows under the harsh yoke of repression."

The Control Voice,
The Outer Limits

❖

"THRUSH believes in the two-party system: The masters and the slaves."

Napoleon Solo,
The Man from U.N.C.L.E.

"Humor is the very essence of a democratic society."

Saying in the Village,
The Prisoner

"In every revolution, there's a man with a vision."

Captain Kirk,
Star Trek

"A cardinal rule of poli-
tics—never get caught in
bed with a live man or a
dead woman."

J.R. Ewing,
Dallas

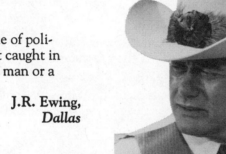

"On Ork, if someone wants to be president, we just say, sure, go
ahead, it's cool."

Mork,
Mork and Mindy

"I couldn't be President. I don't even know who we're fighting."

Six-year-old,
Art Linkletter's House Party

"Any Democrat is mentally ill."

Victor Isbecki,
Cagney & Lacey

❖

Olive Oyl: "Popeye, why don't women run for president?"
Popeye: "'Cause they're too busy running for husbands."

Popeye,
The Popeye Cartoon Show

❖

"As my old grandpappy used to say, one man's political persuasion is another man's prison sentence."

Ben Maverick,
Young Maverick

❖

"Politicians have to fight on those panel shows, or they wouldn't be funny, and no one would watch the programs."

Wally Cleaver,
Leave It to Beaver

❖

Agent 99: "Couldn't we just ask the government for help?"
Maxwell Smart: "We just can't go running to them every time we have a little problem."
99: "Well, what about Congress, Max—they could put in a special appropriation."
Max: "Well, how long would that take?"
99: "Three months."
Max: "Well, what if it was an emergency?"
99: "Four months."

Get Smart

❖

"When I was in third grade, there was a kid running for office. His slogan was: 'Vote for me and I'll show you my wee-wee.' He won by a landslide."

Dorothy,
The Golden Girls

Postmortem

Lou Grant: "Not much of a crowd here."
Ted Baxter: "I know. If it were my funeral, this place would be packed."
Murray Slaughter: "That's right, Ted. It's just a matter of giving the public what they want."

The Mary Tyler Moore Show

❖

Jim Rockford: "Angel, I have a funeral to attend."
Angel: "So what if you're late? The guest of honor will notice?"

The Rockford Files

❖

"There is nothing quite so good as a burial at sea. It is simple, tidy, and not very incriminating."

Alfred Hitchcock,
Alfred Hitchcock Presents

❖

"I don't want anybody to make a fuss. When I go, I just want to be stood outside in the garbage with my hat on."

Lou Grant,
The Mary Tyler Moore Show

❖

"I'd rather go out in a blaze of hydrocarbons than provide a cheap source of protein for the world's invertebrates."

David Addison,
Moonlighting

❖

"Martin Levine has passed away at the age of seventy-five. Mr. Levine had owned a movie-theater chain here in New York. The funeral will be held on Thursday, at 2:15, 4:20, 6:30, 8:40, and 10:50."

David Letterman,
Late Night with David Letterman

Poverty

"I'm a poor man. I even have no right to be fat!"

Sgt. Hans Shultz,
Hogan's Heroes

❖

"Mostly, it's been my sad fate to look on the fine art of spending as strictly a spectator sport."

Dobie Gillis,
The Many Loves of Dobie Gillis

❖

Sgt. Ernie Bilko: "You got a raise to forty-two dollars a week and you've been with them nineteen years?"
Twinhazy: "Next year I get a gold watch."
Bilko: "So you can time the hunger pains?"

The Phil Silvers Show

❖

Lamont Sanford: "I can't stand it here. I can't stand being poor."
Fred Sanford: "Poor? When I was a kid, we slept seven in one bed—same bed, same underwear. When I was a youngster, I wore one pair of tennis shoes five years—wore them up to the name on the ankle. Now that's poor. You're in the lap of luxury here."

Sanford and Son

❖

"So what if I'm not sitting in the lap of luxury? I'm happy where I am, on the bony knees of nothing."

Lucy Ricardo,
I Love Lucy

❖

Florence Johnston: "I ain't got no money."
George Jefferson: "I just paid you a full week's salary."
Florence: "I know. I blew it all on a pay toilet."

The Jeffersons

❖

Lovey Howell: "You know, I really wouldn't mind being poor, if it weren't for one thing."
Thurston Howell III: "What is that, my dear?"
Lovey: "Poverty."

Gilligan's Island

The Power of Money

South American politician: "Breeding certainly tells, doesn't it?"
Cinnamon Carter: "Yes, but unfortunately money dictates."

Mission: Impossible

❖

"The world runs on money. Everybody walks around with this invisible number in their heads. You hit the figure close enough, the penny drops. You own the man."

Ray,
Stingray

❖

"A golden key opens every lock, Robin."

Batman,
Batman

❖

"Money can't buy happiness. . . . But then, happiness can't buy government-insured C.D.'s."

David Addison,
Moonlighting

❖

[Batman and Robin are hanging precariously over a cauldron of boiling wax.]
Robin: "Holy paraffin, Batman! This is going to be a close one!"
Batman: "Too close!"
Riddler: "This is my dream come true! With you two out of the way, nothing can stand between me and the Lost Treasure of the

Incas . . . and it's worth millions . . . millions! Hear me Batman? *Millions!*"

Batman: "Just remember, Riddler, you can't buy friends with money."

Batman

❖

"Gold is human honey, man. Draws flies."

Alexander Scott,
I Spy

Practical Advice

"Always keep your bowler on in times of stress—and a watchful eye open for diabolical masterminds!"

Emma Peel,
The Avengers

❖

Bailey Porter: "I planned my high school homecoming parade once. The only thing I can remember is: Never put the horses up front."
Venus Flytrap: "Why? Oh, yeah."

WKRP in Cincinnati

❖

"The first thing to do when you're being stalked by an angry mob with raspberries is to release a tiger."

John Cleese,
Monty Python's Flying Circus

❖

Mark Harris (preparing to return to the ocean): "I'm going to tell you something now, and I want you to listen. . . . "
Dr. Elizabeth Merrill: "Well, what?"
Mark: "Keep your ears clean, Elizabeth."

The Man from Atlantis

❖

"When on Earth, do as the Earthlings."

Mork,
Mork and Mindy

❖

"When you handle yourself, use your head; when you handle others, use your heart."

Donna Reed,
The Donna Reed Show

"When you want something done, go to the busy man. He's the one who'll find time to do it."

Jim Anderson,
Father Knows Best

❖

"Always enter a strange hotel room with extreme caution, especially one with a samurai warrior in it."

Thomas Magnum,
Magnum, P.I.

❖

"Swallow what's bitter in the cup and move on."

Howard Hunter,
Hill Street Blues

❖

" 'Don't worry' is good advice. All you get is gray hair and more wrinkles."

Huggy Bear,
Starsky and Hutch

❖

"If you can't fight 'em, and they won't let you join 'em, best get out of the county."

Pappy Maverick,
Maverick

❖

"Just keep laughin'."

Bozo the Clown,
Bozo's Circus

Pregnancy

"I know it's one of life's pleasures to carry another human being, but I've been doing it for nine months and I wish the little bugger would get off the stick!"

Georgette Baxter,
The Mary Tyler Moore Show

❖

"I never realized the last stage of pregnancy could be so stimulating! Almost as stimulating as the first!"

Sue Anne Nivens,
The Mary Tyler Moore Show

❖

Julie Kotter: "Stop treating pregnancy as if it were a disease!"
Juan Epstein: "My mother thinks it is. She got pregnant eight times. Now, she's taken to wearing garlic—and my father's taken to sleeping on the roof."

Welcome Back, Kotter

Pride

"Pride is a funny thing: Swallow a little or swallow a lot—it all tastes the same."

Tod Stiles,
Route 66

❖

Ralph Kramden: "I promise you this, Norton. I'm gonna learn. I'm gonna learn from here on in how to swallow my pride."
Ed Norton: "That ought not to be too hard. You've learned how to swallow everything else."

The Honeymooners

Prison

Big Mike: "While I was in solitary, I spent a lotta time thinkin'. I did a lot of thinkin'. I thought about the walls . . . the bars . . . the guards with the guns. You know what I figured out?"
Other Con: "What?"
Big Mike: "We're in prison."

Your Show of Shows

❖

"A man confined to prison is a man who has given up his liberty, his pursuit of happiness. No more carefree hours, no more doing whatever you want, whenever you want. No more peanut butter and jelly sandwiches."

Barney Fife,
The Andy Griffith Show

❖

Beth Davenport (an attorney): "Don't you think she's innocent?"
Jim Rockford: "I spent five years in prison. I never met anybody there who wasn't innocent."

The Rockford Files

Psychiatry

"There's nothing to be afraid of. You have a stomach ache, you go to a doctor, right? You have a toothache, you go to a dentist. You have primary and secondary ego diffusion, you go to a psychiatrist."

Alex Reiger,
Taxi

❖

Harry Von Zell: "George needs somebody who understands these cases, and I know just the man . . . he has hundreds of nervous patients."
Gracie Allen: "He can't be so good if he makes all his patients nervous."

The George Burns and Gracie Allen Show

❖

Doctor: "The trouble with psychologists is that we're stuck in a rut. All we do is repeat ourselves."
Bob Hartley: "Repeat ourselves?"
Doctor: "Repeat ourselves."
Bob: "How?"
Doctor: "How?"
Bob: "Yeah—how?"
Doctor: "By using the same old methods, over and over and over again and again and again and again."
Bob: "I see what you mean."

The Bob Newhart Show

❖

T.V. interviewer: "You mean, you ask forty dollars an hour and you guarantee nothing?"
Bob Hartley: "Well, I validate."

The Bob Newhart Show

The Pyramids

"Can you imagine pilin' up all them rocks just to bury yourself?"

Hoss Cartwright,
Bonanza

Questions and Answers

> "Questions are a burden to others, answers a prison for oneself."
>
> **Sign in the Village,**
> *The Prisoner*

❖

Laura Holt: "Some questions are best left unanswered."
Remington Steele: "And some answers are best left unquestioned."
> *Remington Steele*

Raising Kids

> "You know, one of these days daughters may go out of style. Fathers won't be able to afford them."
>
> **Jim Anderson,**
> *Father Knows Best*

❖

Fred McConnell: "My daughter . . . *my* daughter . . . is living with a man."
Cop: "Mindy? Oh, come on."
Fred: "It's true, it's true, she's a loose woman and I don't know how to tighten her."
> *Mork and Mindy*

❖

> "I'm glad we don't have a girl. Our staircase isn't wide enough for her to throw her bridal bouquet from."
>
> **June Cleaver,**
> *Leave It to Beaver*

❖

Nick: "You see, we have this slight philosophical difference here concerning discipline. Annie doesn't think you should force kids to do things."
Annie: "If you force a child to do something, he'll never love it."
Nick: "There's a lot of things children have to do whether they love

it or not."

Annie: "But if they could love it, they'd do it better."

Nick: "Yeah, but if they don't love it, they won't do it, so you have to force them."

Annie: "But if you force the child to do it, then you'll never know if they could love it."

Nick: "Well, they might find out they love it because you forced them."

Annie: "You're right."

Nick: "I am?"

Annie: "No, but we have guests."

Annie McGuire

❖

Fred Sanford: "Didn't you learn anything being my son? Who do you think I'm doing this all for?"

Lamont Sanford: "Yourself."

Fred: "Yeah, you learned something."

Sanford and Son

❖

Mr. Hilliard: "Mr. Addams, surely you want your youngsters to be like other children?"

Gomez Addams: "But they are. You should see Pugsley wrestling with his octopus."

The Addams Family

❖

Sophia: "She's always tellin' me what to do!"

Rocco: "Don't worry. My daughter treats me the same way."

Sophia: "Kids. Once they're over fifty, they think they know everything."

The Golden Girls

Reading

"I like to read. It's a lot of fun when you know how!"

Pee-Wee Herman,
Pee-Wee's Playhouse

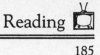
❖

Miss Hathaway: "Do you like Kipling?"
Jethro Bodine: "I don't know—I ain't never kippled."
The Beverly Hillbillies

❖

"I read a book twice as fast as anybody else. First I read the beginning, and then I read the ending, and then I start in the middle and read toward whichever end I like best."
Gracie Allen,
The George Burns and Gracie Allen Show

❖

Hoss Cartwright: "I thought you told me you were gonna try to get some sleep!"
Adam Cartwright: "Well, I tried, but I couldn't. I was just reading something by Mr. Thoreau. 'The mass of men lead lives of quiet desperation. What one trusts to be truths turn into compromises, and what is called resignation, is confirmed desperation.' "
Hoss: "Yeah. Pretty sour pill to have to take, ain't it? But I guess it's the truth. Reckon that's why me and books just always were in a different world."
Bonanza

❖

"You know something? If you couldn't read, you couldn't look up what was on television."
Beaver Cleaver,
Leave It to Beaver

❖

"This paperback is very interesting, but I find it will never replace a hardcover book—it makes a very poor doorstop."
Alfred Hitchcock,
Alfred Hitchcock Presents

❖

"Moonlight is romantic but it's hell to read by."

Remington Steele,
Remington Steele

❖

"What you like about a book goes on forever because it becomes part of you."

Starman,
Starman

❖

"Wilbur, beat me, take away my food, my water, my TV, but don't take away my comic books."

Mr. Ed,
Mr. Ed

Relationships

"Even a lousy passionate relationship is better than no passion at all."
Arnie Becker,
L.A. Law

❖

"When you care for someone . . . I mean really care for them . . . you don't try to change them. . . . You take the good with the bad and be thankful for what you've got."

Tony Nelson,
I Dream of Jeannie

❖

"I have never understood why it is necessary to become irrational in order to prove that you care, or why it should be necessary to prove it at all."

Kerr Avon,
Blake's 7

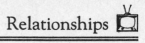
❖

"It's very difficult to maintain a relationship based solely on mistrust."
Remington Steele,
Remington Steele

❖

"I'm looking for a serious commitment—someone who'll stay the night."

Stewardess,
Married ...with Children

❖

"I don't want to go day-to-day. I'm not a Kelly Girl. I want a commitment."

Judy,
The Slap Maxwell Story

❖

Frank Burns: "Why does everyone take an instant dislike to me?"
Trapper John McIntire: "It saves time, Frank."

M*A*S*H

❖

"Sometimes you have to get to know someone really well to realize you're really strangers."

Mary Richards,
The Mary Tyler Moore Show

❖

"You're really letting me down as a boyfriend, not being able to control the weather and all."

Stephanie Vanderkellan,
Newhart

❖

Louie DePalma: "I like Zena. . . . I really do . . . but I can't even bring myself to kiss her."

Alex Reiger [sarcastically]: "Well, there's only one thing you can do Louie—break up with this lovely, warm person who obviously feels a great deal for you and spend the rest of your life floating through meaningless affairs with cheap strangers who you'll have to pay to satisfy your disgusting physical lust!"
Louie [relieved]: "Great advice!"

Taxi

❖

Emily Hartley: "Bob, do you love me?"
Bob Hartley: "Sure."
Emily: "Why?"
Bob: "Why not?"

The Bob Newhart Show

❖

"I know we've never been friends. I could never relate to someone who cuts the crusts off their bread."

Mrs. Fein,
Soap

Responsibility

"A man does what he has to do—if he can't get out of it."

Pappy Maverick,
Maverick

❖

"Dig right in and do it now, whatever should be done.
You're a dope to sit and mope, when everything is fun."
Mouseketeer Tommy [singing with Jimmy Dodd]
The Mickey Mouse Club

❖

Eddie Haskell [to Wally Cleaver]: "Work in the yard? Aw, come off it! We got—oh, good morning, Mr. and Mrs. Cleaver."
June Cleaver: "Hello, Eddie."
Ward Cleaver: "Good morning, Eddie."

Eddie: "Well, if you've got work to do, Wallace, I don't want to interfere. I was reading an article in the paper the other day where a certain amount of responsibility around the home was good character training. Goodbye, Mr. and Mrs. Cleaver."

Leave It to Beaver

Revenge

Sue Ellen Ewing: "You've already ruined his career. . . . Isn't that enough?"

J.R. Ewing: "Hell, no."

Dallas

❖

"Now you go to Supreme Salvage and pick up some bathtubs I ordered. Here's a check. Now listen, if you try to run off with my truck and try to cash my check, I'll find you. It may take a week, it may take a month, it might take me years, but one day—maybe fifty years from now—you'll be walkin' down the street and, when you least expect it, a hundred-fifteen-year-old man gonna jump out of the alley with a two-by-four and cave your skull in."

Fred Sanford,
Sanford and Son

❖

Sam: "Let me give you some advice, Carla. I suggest you turn the other cheek."
Carla: "Mooning her isn't enough—I want to hurt her!"

Cheers

❖

"That man robbed me! *Robbed* me! I had revenge in my heart. Revenge! Revenge is sweet . . . but I'm trying to cut down."

New York victim,
Barney Miller

The Rich

[To Mama's rich boyfriend] "It's a pleasure to meet a man of your charming credit rating."

Kingfish,
Amos 'n' Andy

❖

"He's got a purse the size of an elephant's scrotum, and it's just as hard to get your hands on."

Edmund Blackadder,
Blackadder II

❖

Mrs. Fenwick: "Your banker tells me you're worth forty million dollars. Why do you drive around in that truck and dress as you do and eat grits and hog jowls?"
Jed Clampett: "Well, the way I look at it, Widow, if ya got it, spend it!"

The Beverly Hillbillies

❖

"Wealth is the only reality."

Kerr Avon,
Blake's 7

❖

"As my Great Aunt Maude always said, to own a priceless treasure one must first be worthy of it."

Artemus Gordon,
The Wild, Wild West

Romance

"Gomez, I've been yours since that first day you carved my initials in your leg."

Morticia Addams,
The Addams Family

❖

"A girl likes a little sweet talk, you know. It's plastic, but we love it!"

Girl,
The Odd Couple

❖

Woman: "When a boy kisses a girl and she says 'Stop,' she usually means 'Stop it. I love it.' And it was sort of like that."
Groucho Marx: "You mean when a girl says 'Stop,' she really means 'Don't stop'? Boy, the nights I've wasted. I was always so gullible."

You Bet Your Life

❖

"In that great furnace known as romance, your pilot light's gone out."

Grandpa,
The Munsters

Rules of Etiquette

"You don't want your hands full when you say hello."

Starman,
Starman

❖

Mindy McConnell: "It's not nice to sit on your face."
Mork: "Then why did God put it there?"

Mork and Mindy

❖

"Herman, show some respect for tonight's guest of honor; why don't you go upstairs and change your socks?"

Grandpa Munster,
The Munsters

❖

"Proper young ladies do not enter houses behind a barrage of machine-gun bullets."

Bud Anderson,
Father Knows Best

❖

"You don't use a fork with soup."

Sam Malone,
Cheers

❖

"You should always turn your head when you sneeze at the table, but you'd better grab your plate and take it with you, because then people can't sneak vegetables on your plate that you don't want while your head's turned."

Kid,
Art Linkletter's House Party

❖

Girl: "You've just put the lighted end of the cigarette in your mouth!"
Maxwell Smart: "Yes, that way I don't get too many ashes on the carpet."

Get Smart

❖

"Sending assassins to kill me is in very poor taste."

Illya Kuryakin,
The Man from U.N.C.L.E.

"We don't go around yanking other men's ex-wives' upper arms."

Felix Unger,
The Odd Couple

Rules to Live By

"If you can make the other guy feel like a goon first, *you* don't feel like so much of a goon."

Eddie Haskell,
Leave It to Beaver

❖

"Never go to jail without your hat. That's a rule."

Rick Simon,
Simon and Simon

❖

"Let me tell you girls the three most important things I learned about life. Number one: hold fast to your friends. Number two: there's no

such thing as security. Number three: don't go see *Ishtar*."

Sophia,
The Golden Girls

❖

"Interfere? Of course we should interfere. Always do what you're best at, I always say."

Doctor Who,
Doctor Who

❖

"As my Great Aunt Maude always told me, never hitch your wagon to another man's star. You never know where the fool will take you."

Artemus Gordon,
The Wild ,Wild West

❖

"Like my old skleenball coach used to say, 'Find out what you don't do well, then don't do it.'"

Alf,
ALF

❖

"Working rule number twenty-three: Go through the motions anyway; you might get lucky."

Thomas Magnum,
Magnum P.I.

❖

"Bernstein's rule number one: Never flirt with a woman whose husband carries a gun."

Irwin Bernstein,
Hill Street Blues

❖

"A man is less likely to kill on a full stomach."

Victoria Barkley,
The Big Valley

❖

"When you make a mistake, admit it. If you don't, you only make matters worse."

Ward Cleaver,
Leave It to Beaver

"A watched cauldron never bubbles."

Morticia Addams,
The Addams Family

❖

"As far as possible without surrender, be on good terms with all."

Caine,
Kung Fu

❖

"As we say in the sewer, if you're not prepared to go all the way, don't put your boots on in the first place."

Ed Norton,
The Honeymooners

❖

"Mr. Bill's Law: 'If anything bad can happen to you, then stay away from me, because I'll probably get it too.'"

Mr. Bill,
Saturday Night Live

❖

"If you let your hair down, you might be surprised what you find in it."
Balki Bartokomous,
Perfect Strangers

❖

"Don't feed a starving man a big dinner. Give him a little bit at a time."

A pastor,
Crossroads

❖

"Be kind to the people you meet on the way up, because you're going to meet the same people on the way down."
Ralph Kramden,
The Honeymooners

❖

"If I've told you once, I've told you a thousand times—integrity doesn't feed the bulldog."

Larry Tate,
Bewitched

Science

"Science and ego make lousy chemistry."
Dr. Louis Walker,
Thriller

❖

"Science is a matter of trial and error."
Dr. Smith,
Lost in Space

❖

Astronomy

"Space is big—*really* big."

Text from *The Hitchhiker's Guide,*
The Hitchhiker's Guide to the Galaxy

❖

Biology

Bob Hartley: "When I was in pre-med, and I was taking biology, I found out I'd have to kill a frog and dissect it. I couldn't do it, so I just let it go out the window."
Carol Bondurant: "Well, that was the humane thing to do."
Bob: "Of course, we were eight stories up."
Carol: "Oh, my God."
Bob: "That's what the guy in the convertible said."

The Bob Newhart Show

❖

Chemistry

Aesop, Jr. : "There's no *fuel* like an old *fuel!*"
Aesop, Sr.: "Hmmm. . . . I *gas* you're right."

The Bullwinkle Show

❖

"Chrome wasn't built in a day."

Aesop, Jr.,
The Bullwinkle Show

❖

Genetics

"The roots of physical aggression found in the male species are in the DNA molecule itself. In fact, the very letters DNA are an acronym for 'Dames are Not Aggressors.' "

Cliff Clavin,
Cheers

❖

Physics

"A dog can't get struck by lightning. You know why? 'Cause he's too close to the ground. See, lightning strikes tall things. Now, if they were giraffes out there in that field, now then we'd be in trouble. But you sure don't have to worry about dogs."

Barney Fife,
The Andy Griffith Show

❖

"This may defy the law of gravity, but I never studied law."

Bugs Bunny,
The Bugs Bunny Show

❖

"As Isaac Newton said as the apple fell on his head: 'Strange, I'm sitting under a pear tree!' "

Laugh-In

❖

Harry Von Zell: "Gracie, isn't that boiling water you're putting in the refrigerator?"
Gracie Allen: "Yes, I'm freezing it."
Harry: "You're freezing it?"
Gracie: "Um hmm, and then whenever I want boiling water, all I have to do is defrost it."

The George Burns and Gracie Allen Show

❖

Admiral Nelson: "I say we can stop the fire by exploding a nuclear device three thousand miles in the air. This will blow the burning gases clear of the Earth's magnetic field."
Scientist: "That sounds like a dangerous plan!"

Voyage to the Bottom of the Sea

❖

"There are atmospheric rays that control bodily motion. Now if a person containing a negative or hexum qualities gets between you and those rays, why, then, he creates a static that jars any successful motion into an unsuccessful motion and jinxes you. And that is a scientific fact."

Barney Fife,
The Andy Griffith Show

Self-Defense

"You can be a gentleman and still not forget all you know about self-defense."

Pappy Maverick,
Maverick

❖

"Don't say 'but' when you're fighting for your life."

Simon Templar,
The Saint

❖

"Perceive the way of nature and no force of men can harm you. Do not meet a wave head on, avoid it. You do not have to stop force; it is easier to redirect it."

A monk,
Kung Fu

Sex

"Sex is the major cause of babies."

Trapper John McIntyre,
Trapper John, M.D.

❖

"With my first husband, it was like a news bulletin: brief, unexpected, and usually a disaster."

Mary Campbell,
Soap

❖

"If sex were fast food, you'd have an arch over your head."

Carlotta Winchester,
Filthy Rich

❖

Christine Jorgenson (a famous transexual): "Sex is not determined by genitals alone."
Dick Cavett: "I don't think I quite grasp that . . . . I'm sorry, that's an awful thing to say."

The Dick Cavett Show

❖

Dorothy: "Have you ever felt like you're stuck in a rut, going through the motions with . . . with no joy, or pleasure, or excitement?"
Sophia: "Sure. That was my sex life with your father."

The Golden Girls

❖

"Nothing brings out the woman in the woman more than the man in the man."

Gomez Addams,
The Addams Family

❖

[After his first sexual experience] "I'm so excited. . . . It's like discovering America, or a third arm or something. . . . This is the greatest thing that ever happened to me. I should have started this ten years ago. . . . I mean, the hell with television."

Billy Tate,
Soap

❖

"I guess I'm old-fashioned—I wouldn't sleep with a guy unless we were living together."

Barbara Cooper,
One Day at a Time

❖

Sue Ann Nivens [as they leave the table]: "What's that expression—a great meal is the prelude to a symphony of lovemaking?"
Lou Grant: "Who said that?"
Sue Ann [as she corners him on the couch]: "I did."

The Mary Tyler Moore Show

❖

"I haven't had much experience saying 'No' to a woman. The closest I've ever come is, 'Not now, we're landing.' "

Sam Malone,
Cheers

❖

"Can robot lips do this?"

Alien woman,
Star Trek

❖

Sam Malone: "I thought you weren't going to call me stupid now that we're being intimate."
Diane Chambers: "No, I said I wasn't going to call you stupid *while* we were being intimate."

Cheers

Sex Education

Mrs. Kotter: "We're trying to teach kids that sex is not disgusting."
Mrs. Zugler: "I've been married for twenty-seven years—don't tell *me* what's disgusting!"

Welcome Back, Kotter

❖

"Sex in the hands of public educators is not a pretty thing."

Kevin Arnold,
The Wonder Years

❖

Marian Cunningham: "In California, they teach the birds and the bees right in school."
Howard Cunningham: "That's California, this is Milwaukee. The birds and the bees are only here four months out of the year."

Happy Days

Sexual Confusion

Little Girl: "I'm wearing pants—but I'm a *girl!*"
Allen Funt: "A girl?"
Little Girl: "Do I have hair like you?"
Funt: "No."
Little Girl: "Well, *that* means I'm not a boy—if I don't have very short hair I'm not a boy."
Funt: "If I let my hair grow long like yours, would I be a girl then?"
Little Girl: "Yes—if you keep brushing it."

Candid Camera

❖

Victim's Grieving Widow: "Do you know what it's like to be married to a wonderful man for fourteen years?"
Det. Drebin: "No, I can't say that I do. I did . . . uh . . . live with a guy once, though, but that was just for a couple of years. The usual slurs, rumors, innuendoes—people didn't understand."

Police Squad !

❖

Nurse: "Why in the world would you want to have a sex change operation?"
Patient: "I hear women live longer."

Soap

❖

"You can point to any item in the Sears catalog and somebody wants to sleep with it."

Det. Stanley Wojohowicz,
Barney Miller

❖

Judy: Men!"
Dutch: "The trouble is, what else you got?"
Slap: "That's it. I mean, we are the only game in town."
Judy: "Maybe. Maybe not."
Dutch: "Let me see, that would leave. . . . "
Slap: "Well, don't even think about that, Dutch."
Judy: "Women are just nicer human beings. It's a biological fact."
Dutch: "You never met *my* missus."
Slap: "Now, we are, uh, just making conversation here, right? I mean, this is not in the realm of actual consideration."
Judy: "Anything's possible."
Slap: "Okay, all right. It's your call. But listen, if you decide to, can I—can I watch? [pause] I'm sorry. *May* I watch?"

The Slap Maxwell Story

Shopping

Steven Keaton: "Mallory, reading is one of the greatest joys of life. When you were young you used to read all the time. What happened?"
Mallory Keaton: "I discovered shopping."

Family Ties

❖

Mary Beth Lacey: "Men don't understand shopping."
Chris Cagney: "I think it's genetic."

Cagney & Lacey

❖

"You know, I've never really noticed how beautiful a supermarket could be."

Contestant,
Supermarket Sweep

❖

Mallory Keaton: "I don't go to the mall that much.
Alex Keaton: "Mallory, the mannequins *wave* at you."

Family Ties

Siblings

Mallory Keaton: "So you believe in the old double standard then, don't you?"
Alex Keaton: "No, no, I believe in a triple standard: one for girls, one for boys, and one for sisters."

Family Ties

❖

Maddie Hayes: "I didn't know you had a brother."
David Addison: "I never thought of him as a brother, I thought of him as Mom and Dad's science project."

Moonlighting

❖

Mindy McConnell: "Brothers are almost always male."
Mork: "Not Dr. Joyce Brothers."

Mork and Mindy

❖

Bobby Ewing: "I'm still your brother."
J.R. Ewing: "My brother? As far as I'm concerned, I'm an only child."

Dallas

❖

Rick Simon: "This is my brother, A.J."
Lolita: "Same father?"
Rick: "Same father, different mood."

Simon and Simon

❖

Larry Appleton: "Why shouldn't I resent you? When I was a kid Mom and Dad always said, 'Why can't you be more like your brother, the athlete?' "
Billy Appleton: "How about me? They always said, 'Why can't you get grades like your brother's?' "

Larry: "Gosh, you mean we spent our childhood resenting each other when we should have been resenting *them?*"

Perfect Strangers

❖

Frank Hardy: "You're holding up pretty good for a younger brother."
Joe Hardy: "It's your example I'm trying to live down to."

The Hardy Boys

Silence

"If you can't say anything—don't."

Hilaire Tattinger,
Tattinger's

❖

"When words are no better than silences, one should keep silent."

Caine,
Kung Fu

❖

"A still tongue makes a happy life."

Saying in the Village,
The Prisoner

Sin

Louie Wilson: "Name the seven deadly sins."
Chico Rodriguez: "Uh, greed, lust—that's my own personal favorite—avarice, uh . . . and Sleepy, Doc and Grumpy?"

Chico and the Man

❖

Eccentric Rich Woman: "The wages of sin is death! Thou shalt not commit adultery! Do you know who said that?"
Jake Axminster: "DeMille?"

The City of Angels

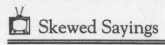
Skewed Sayings

"You've buttered your bread, now sleep in it."

Gracie Allen,
The George Burns and Gracie Allen Show

❖

"Remember what Shakespeare said: 'East is East and West is West, and you're all right as long as the trains don't meet.'"

Andy,
Amos 'n' Andy

"An ounce of prevention is worth a pound of bandages and adhesive tape."

Groucho Marx,
You Bet Your Life

❖

"It's like looking for a needle in a hayride!"

Archie Bunker,
All in the Family

❖

"One who fights fire with fire only gets in trouble with Smokey the Bear."

Herman Munster,
The Munsters

❖

"Ours is not to reason why, ours is but to do and become permanently deactivated."

The Robot,
Lost in Space

❖

"People in stucco houses should not throw quiche."

Sonny Crockett,
Miami Vice

❖

Dan: "Ask not for whom the bell tolls."
Roseanne: "It tolls for thee, Butthead."

Roseanne

Sleep

Martin Kazinski: "Speaking of sleep. . . . "
Malloy: "Y'know, I did that once and twenty-four hours later I was tired again.

Kaz

❖

Interviewer: "Doctor, would you explain to the audience in simple language the basis for your theory on sleep?"
Dr. Sigfried von Sedative (Sid Caesar): "Sleep is wonderful. Sleep is beautiful. But sleep is no good if you're wide awake."

Your Show of Shows

Spiritual Pursuits

Sister Allison: "You're not religious, are you?"
Ray: "I am, in my own way. I've seen a lot of evil—here, all over the world—the horror of war, injustice. If I have a religion, I guess my religion is my belief in the inherent good in all people, and having faith in that belief. Sometimes it takes all the strength that I have."

Stingray

❖

"You have to believe in the gods to see them."

Hopi the Indian,
Gumby

❖

"I'm going to take the moment to contemplate most of the Western religions. I'm looking for something soft on morality, generous with holidays, and with a very short initiation period."

David Addison,
Moonlighting

❖

"Let's leave religion to the televangelists. After all, they're the professionals."

Cheviot,
Max Headroom

❖

"We in the spirit game have a saying: What you don't know can hurt you a whole lot."

Dr. Clove,
The Odd Couple

❖

"Never make friends with the devil, brother; his pitchfork will get you in the end."

Artemus Gordon,
The Wild, Wild West

❖

"I meditated for hours on end. Chanted. I was finding God all over the place. He kept ditching me. You gotta understand, I thought I was on my way to Nirvana. All I ended up with was recurrent flashbacks of the original Mouseketeers."

Reverend Jim Ignatowski,
Taxi

❖

"The pilgrims who drink the water of the Ganges shall trot all the way to the mosque."

Laugh-In

❖

"Edith, Sunday's supposed to be the day of rest. How can I rest when I'm going to church?"

Archie Bunker,
All in the Family

Sports

"You guys were slinging so much bull I was afraid you'd get buried in it. I guess that's what sports is. Bull."

Elliot Maxwell,
The Slap Maxwell Story

❖

"What's more important, bowling or watching your kid rot?"

Oscar Madison,
The Odd Couple

❖

[A boxer, dressed in robe and trunks, sits in a corner blowing on a saxophone. Det. Drebin suddenly grabs it from him.]
"I told you, no sax before a fight."

Det. Frank Drebin,
Police Squad!

❖

"I never play horseshoes, 'cause Mother taught us not to throw our clothes around."

Mr. Ed,
Mr. Ed

❖

College Chancellor: "Gentlemen, Bullwinkle Moose is the greatest football player since Blue Grange."
Professor: "Isn't that *Red* Grange, Chancellor?"
Chancellor: "Let's not get controversial."

The Bullwinkle Show

❖

"The game of football is played all over the world. In some countries, such a game may be called a soccer match. In others, a revolution. However, there are several differences between a football game and a revolution. For one thing, a football game usually lasts longer and the participants wear uniforms. Also, there are usually more casualties in a football game. The object of the game is to move a ball past the other team's goal line. This counts as six points. No points are given for lacerations, contusions, or abrasions, but then no points are deducted, either. Kicking is very important in football. In fact, some of the more enthusiastic players even kick the football occasionally."

Alfred Hitchcock,
Alfred Hitchcock Presents

"Tennis is a young man's game. Until you're twenty-five, you can play singles. From twenty-five to thirty-five, you should play doubles. I won't tell you exactly how old I am, but when I played, there were twenty-eight men on the court—just on my side of the net."

George Burns,
The George Burns and Gracie Allen Show

❖

"I've got a theory about why you Limeys are so batty about soccer. It's a good excuse to watch all these young boys run around in short pants."

Chalmers,
Remington Steele

❖

Lois Lane [mooning over Superman]: "Clark, does spring mean anything to you?"
Clark Kent: "Baseball."
Lois: "Do you think spring means anything to Superman?"
Clark: "He doesn't have time for baseball!"

The Adventures of Superman

Stand Up and Fight Like a Man

"The true test of a warrior is not without. It is within. It is here, here inside that we must meet the challenge. It is the weaknesses within here that a warrior must overcome."

Worf,
Star Trek: The Next Generation

❖

Farrah: "A swordsman does not fear death if he dies with honor."
Doctor Who: "Then he's an idiot."

Doctor Who

❖

"If all the men who lived by the gun were laid end to end, I wouldn't be surprised."

Pappy Maverick,
Maverick

❖

[Lt. Drebin punches out a man who's pointing a gun at him.]
Admiring Woman: "Say, that was nice work. You took a big chance

doing that."

Lt. Frank Drebin [modestly]: We-e-ell, you take a chance getting out of bed in the morning . . . crossing the street . . . or sticking your face in a fan."

Police Squad!

❖

"To fight for yourselves is right. But to die vainly without hope of winning is the act of stupid men."

Caine,
Kung Fu

❖

"Angry men fight like fools."

Sir Lancelot,
The Adventures of Sir Lancelot

❖

"He who fights and runs away lives to run away another day."

Pappy Maverick,
Maverick

Success and Failure

"If at first you don't succeed—give the whole thing up; no sense in making a fool of yourself."

Susanna Pomeroy,
The Gale Storm Show

❖

Mel Sharples: "My brother's doing so well in the used car business, he can afford all three of his divorces."
Alice Hyatt: "That's success."

Alice

❖

"If at first you don't succeed, try something else."

Pappy Maverick,
Maverick

❖

"If you're going to be a failure, you might as well be a success at it."

Bud Anderson,
Father Knows Best

❖

"There's nothing like failure to dry up the money supply."

Space Traveler,
Space:1999

Suicide

"I don't believe in suicide—it stunts your growth."

Vila Restal,
Blake's 7

Superstition

George Jefferson: "Get away from the mirror—you don't need any more bad luck."
Florence Johnston: "I know. I already got you."

The Jeffersons

❖

"In my country there is a belief—and rightly so—that the only thing separating us from the animals is mindless superstitions and pointless rituals."

Latka Gravis,
Taxi

❖

"Some superstitions, kept alive by the long night of ignorance, have their own special power."

Rod Serling,
The Twilight Zone

❖

"How can I have so much bad luck with four horseshoes?"

Mr. Ed,
Mr. Ed

Sushi

Amy Cassidy: "Henry, do you want to have lunch with me? I'm having sushi."
Henry Desmond: "Raw fish doesn't sound like lunch. It sounds like a fraternity prank."

Bosom Buddies

❖

Nick Yemana: "Japanese got a lot of willpower—we eat raw fish!"
Ron Harris: "You like it."
Nick: "No we don't."

Barney Miller

❖

Elaine [to a foreign visitor]: "Have you tried sushi yet?"
Foreigner: "No, not yet. I don't even have a racquet."

Perfect Strangers

Talent

"Some people possess talent, others are possessed by it. When that happens, a talent becomes a curse."

Rod Serling,
The Twilight Zone

❖

"The first time I saw her perform she was so good I wanted to run up to the stage, put my arms around her—and wring her neck. She just has too much talent!"

Judy Garland,
The Hollywood Palace

❖

"By George, this house is a veritable cesspool of talent."

Gomez Addams,
The Addams Family

Taxes

"The government comes for the regular people first."

Cliff Huxtable,
The Cosby Show

❖

"Don't knock the wages of sin—they're tax-free."

Laugh-In

❖

"Even if you're a baby with money the government takes it away from you."

Wally Cleaver,
Leave It to Beaver

❖

Mr. Drysdale: "It's that time again—time to pay income taxes."
Jed Clampett: "Oh, good. Let's give 'em a little extry this year. I can't spend all the money I've got."

The Beverly Hillbillies

❖

Sgt. Chano Amenguale [arriving at work late]: "I just had a meeting with the I.R.S."

Sgt. Stanley Wojohowicz: "What happened?"
Chano: "I won. . . . "
Wojo: "Congratulations."
Chano: "Yeah. I'm not going to jail, and they're going to let me
  live. . . . But very poorly."

Barney Miller

Teeth

"Always take care of your teeth and yer teeth will take care of you."

Poopdeck Pappy,
The Popeye Cartoon Show

❖

"Be true to your teeth and they won't be false to you."

Soupy Sales,
The Soupy Sales Show

❖

Imogene Coca: "I have a lot of trouble with my teeth, you know. And
  there's a reason for it—lack of calcium."
Sid Caesar: "Oh, that'll do it every time!"
Coca: "I just don't have enough calcium in my system. Lots of people
  don't, you know. There are some people who say it has to do with
  the drinking water. For instance, there's a little town upstate that
  has the most amazing drinking water in the country. Some
  chemical in it that's very necessary for teeth. And would you
  believe it, there's not one person in the town who ever had a
  cavity. They all have perfect teeth! Of course, they're bald. . . . But
  their teeth are perfect."

Your Show of Shows

❖

Andy Taylor: "Ready for bed?"
Opie Taylor: "Yes, Pa."
Andy: "Brush your teeth?"
Opie: "Just feel how wet the toothbrush is."
Andy: "I want to tell you a little story. One time, a long time ago,
  there was this little fella and he never brushed his teeth. Now, you
  may not believe this, but all he'd do is wet his toothbrush. To him,

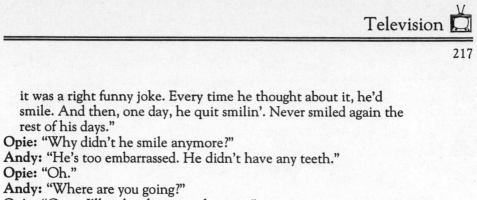
it was a right funny joke. Every time he thought about it, he'd smile. And then, one day, he quit smilin'. Never smiled again the rest of his days."

Opie: "Why didn't he smile anymore?"

Andy: "He's too embarrassed. He didn't have any teeth."

Opie: "Oh."

Andy: "Where are you going?"

Opie: "Guess I'll go brush my teeth again."

The Andy Griffith Show

Television:
Commercials According to Alfred Hitchcock

"As you can see, crime does not pay—even on television. You must have a sponsor."

Alfred Hitchcock,
Alfred Hitchcock Presents

❖

"Of course, just as no rose is complete without thorns, no television show is complete without the following commercial."

Alfred Hitchcock,
Alfred Hitchcock Presents

❖

"When I was a young man, I had an uncle who frequently took me out to dinner. He always accompanied these dinners with minutely

detailed stories about himself. But I listened—because he was paying for the dinner. I don't know why I am reminded of this, but we are about to have one of our commercials."

> Alfred Hitchcock,
> *Alfred Hitchcock Presents*

❖

"Aristotle once said that a play should have a beginning, a middle, and an end. But what did he know? Today, a play must have a first half, a second half, and a station break."

> Alfred Hitchcock,
> *Alfred Hitchcock Presents*

Television: Its Effect

"Television has done much for psychiatry by spreading information about it, as well as contributing to the need for it."

> Alfred Hitchcock,
> *Alfred Hitchcock Presents*

❖

"Television! I'm against it in principle. People huddle around in the dark, straining their eyes while their vocal chords dry up. The very art of conversation is becoming extinct!"

> Stu Erwin,
> *The Trouble with Father*

❖

Ralph Kramden: "Look, Alice, it ain't just the money. There's another reason I don't want no television in this house. It changes people. They stop usin' their brains. They just look. When people get television, they stop readin' books."
Alice Kramden: "Well, it can't change us. We don't even have a book!"
Ralph: "All right. All right. I'll get you a book!"

> *The Honeymooners*

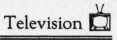
❖

Eddie Munster: "Hey, Mom. Maybe Dad's out playing poker with some men and when he comes home you'll have to yell at him and make him sleep on the sofa."
Lily Munster: "Eddie, where do you get ideas like that?"
Eddie: "From television."

The Munsters

Television: Its Future

"It's just plain foolishness, squattin' all day in front of a little black box, starin' bleary-eyed at people who ain't more than two inches high. It's a passin' fancy, I tell you, like buggy whips and high button shoes."

Grandpa Amos McCoy,
The Real McCoys

❖

"Television is a passing fancy. The last time I turned it on, I was confronted by a singing, dancing seltzer pill named Speedy."

Maj. Charles Emerson Winchester,
*M*A*S*H*

Television: Programming

"This show is ridiculous; I can't recommend this to children. I couldn't even recommend it to a Marine! Parents, you should be ashamed to let your children watch this show. Let 'em read a book, go out and play, watch fruit ripen, anything but this."

Dick Loudon,
Newhart

❖

"No wonder they call television a medium; it's so seldom rare or well-done."

Mighty Mouse,
The New Adventures of Mighty Mouse

❖

"On television, every silver lining has a dark cloud, and our show is no different."

The Bullwinkle Show

❖

"Any schedule without Buddy Ebsen . . . sucks eggs."

George Utley,
Newhart

Television: The Business

"Dealing with network executives is like being nibbled to death by ducks."

Eric Sevareid,
CBS News

❖

" 'Nervous producer' is a redundancy. So is 'complaining producer.' "

Morley Safer,
CBS News

❖

"In our business morals are one thing but ratings are everything."

Network 23 Executive,
Max Headroom

❖

"Imitation is the sincerest form of television."

Mighty Mouse,
The New Adventures of Mighty Mouse

❖

Mary Richards: "If it weren't for the rotten things that happen in this world, we couldn't put on the news show. We should be

grateful to all the people who do those rotten things. We should stop them in the streets and say, 'Thank you, Mr. Mugger. Thank you, Mr. Thief. Thank you, Mr. Maniac.' If it weren't for those people, you and I would be out of jobs. It's a lousy business we're in, Mr. Grant; I quit. I'm going to Africa to work with Schweitzer."
Lou Grant: "Mary, Albert Schweitzer is dead."
Mary: "You see what I mean, Mr. Grant? It's a lousy, lousy world."

The Mary Tyler Moore Show

❖

There's a standard formula for success in the entertainment medium, and that is: Beat it to death if it succeeds."

Ernie Kovacs,
The Ernie Kovacs Show

❖

"You know, one of the most exciting things about doing a weekly television show is just showing up."

Judy Garland,
The Judy Garland Show

❖

Mickey Dolenz: "So this is the world of television."
Peter Tork: "That's funny; it doesn't look like a vast wasteland."

The Monkees

❖

"Captain's log, final entry. We have tried to explore strange new worlds, to seek out new civilizations, to boldly go where no man has gone before. And except for one television network, we have found intelligent life everywhere in the galaxy."

Captain Kirk (John Belushi),
Saturday Night Live

❖

Eddie Munster: "Isn't anything real here?"
TV Producer: "Real? This is television!"

The Munsters

Television: Watching It

George: "Gracie, what do you think of television?"
Gracie: "I think it's wonderful—I hardly ever watch radio anymore."
The George Burns and Gracie Allen Show

❖

Francis: "Gunther, what would you do with the evenings if it wasn't for television?"
Gunther: "Francis, I don't even want to think of it."
Car 54, Where Are You?

❖

"I don't watch television, I have a fireplace."
Martha Dudley,
The Mary Tyler Moore Show

❖

Edith Bunker: "Do you like being alone with me?"
Archie Bunker: "Certainly I like being alone with you. What's on television?"
All in the Family

❖

Maggie Crabtree: "It's four o'clock in the morning, and you're watching a test pattern."
Dave Crabtree: "I know, but I want to see how it ends."
My Mother the Car

❖

"This television camera . . . this is the instrument that takes a picture of my face. And it sends it out all over the country. And millions of people, sitting in front of their sets, looking at me . . . it gives them a chance to say, 'Who's that?'"

Ed Wynn,
The Ed Wynn Show

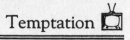
❖

"You needn't stand there staring. We're not going to show you any more. In fact, I'm not even going to tell you what happened. Television audiences are becoming entirely too dependent."

Alfred Hitchcock,
Alfred Hitchcock Presents

❖

Coach Leroy Fedders: "Turn on the TV I wanna watch a cop show."
Blanche Fedders: "Wait a minute. It's time for Monty Hall."
Leroy: "To hell with Monty Hall."
Blanche (horrified): "To *hell* with Monty Hall? But he has such a sincere face, and those sweet eyes!"
Leroy: "I don't care about a sincere face and sweet eyes. I want violence, Blanche!"

Mary Hartman, Mary Hartman

❖

"Hey, Alex—You know the really great thing about television? If something important happens, anywhere in the world, night or day . . . you can always change the channel."

Reverend Jim Ignatowski,
Taxi

Temptation

"The best way to fight temptation is to get rid of it."

Uncle Martin,
My Favorite Martian

❖

"I seen temptation coming, but it seen me coming, too."

Otis Campbell,
The Andy Griffith Show

Theft

Thurston Howell III: "Do you think I began a dozen international corporations by stooping to thievery?"

The Professor: "Well, of course not."
Thurston: "Shows how naive you are. How else do you get to the top of the corporate ladder?"

Gilligan's Island

❖

"One man's theft is another man's justice."

Hawkeye Pierce,
M*A*S*H

❖

Barney Miller: "Don't you understand, you can't go around stealing other people's things."
Purse Snatcher: "If they were mine, why would I want to steal them?"

Barney Miller

❖

"I did a terrible thing. I should have known better. When you steal something, don't ever try to return it."

Maj. Frank Burns,
M*A*S*H

❖

"When you break into a man's office, you should always make it a point to steal something."

Steve McGarrett,
Hawaii Five-0

❖

Gomez Addams: "My dear, did you know that armed robbery is illegal?"
Morticia Addams: "I'm glad, but doesn't that make for unemployment?"
Gomez: "Well, no law is perfect."

The Addams Family

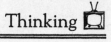
Thinking

"I try not to have any ideas. It only leads to complications."

Johnny Fever,
WKRP in Cincinnati

❖

"It takes a smart man to know he's stupid."

Barney Rubble,
The Flintstones

❖

"If ignorance is bliss, this is Eden."

Diane Chambers,
Cheers

Time

Bob Hartley: "Where does time go?"
Peeper: "Cleveland."

The Bob Newhart Show

❖

"It's hard to believe that a half an hour has gone by when it feels like only thirty minutes."

Kelly Monteith,
The Hit Squad

❖

"Time is very important in television. We buy it, we fill it, we start on it, we must finish on it. And appropriately enough, we occasionally kill it."

Alfred Hitchcock,
Alfred Hitchcock Presents

❖

"A look into the future never gave anyone peace of mind."

Cowboy,
Gunsmoke

❖

"Cling to your youth. Time has a habit of moving forward, never backward, never motionless."

Jim Anderson,
Father Knows Best

Travel

Lucy: "You never take me anywhere."
Ricky: "I never take you anywhere! We just got back from a trip to Europe and last year we went to California."
Lucy: "Yeah, yeah, but where have you taken me lately?"

I Love Lucy

❖

"Where the heck am I, anyway? . . . Well, wherever it is, I don't like it and I'm gettin' outta here."

Bugs Bunny,
The Bugs Bunny Show

❖

Zack: "I might head for parts unknown."
Brodie Hollister: "I been there. The food's terrible."

Bonanza

❖

Rick Simon: "Been out on the road lookin' for America."
A.J. Simon: "Yeah?"
Rick: "It wasn't there."

Simon and Simon

❖

"It's so hard to find a good vacation spot since they closed down Devil's Island."

Lily Munster,
The Munsters

Trust

"Trust is doing something someone asks you to do, even if you think it's dumb."

Starman,
Starman

❖

"A man who trusts can never be betrayed, only mistaken."

Cally,
Blake's 7

❖

Starsky: "Do you trust me or not?"
Hutch: "With my life, yes, with your choice of women, no."

Starsky and Hutch

❖

"I got nothin' against mankind. It's people I don't trust."

Archie Bunker,
All in the Family

❖

"No man is alone. . . .There comes a time when each of us must say, 'I can't do it alone.' Each of us, sooner or later, holds out our hands and says to someone, 'Help me.' When that time comes, all we have left is our trust."

Perry Mason,
Perry Mason

❖

"Once the trust goes out of a relationship, it's really no fun lying to 'em anymore."

Norm Peterson,
Cheers

❖

"I don't trust warm and friendly people."

Lou Grant,
Lou Grant

The Truth

"The steps man takes across the heavens of his universe are as uncertain as those steps he takes across the rooms of his own life. And yet if he walks with an open mind his steps must lead him eventually to that most perfect of all destinations—truth."

The Control Voice,
The Outer Limits

❖

"The truth changes."

Kelly Robinson,
I Spy

❖

Client: "It's the truth. . . . I don't care how bad it sounds."
Perry Mason: "Then don't change a word."

Perry Mason

❖

"Telling the truth would never cramp your style, son. Matter of fact, you tell the truth, it makes your life a lot simpler . . . a lot happier, too."

Danny Williams,
Make Room for Daddy

❖

"You're entitled to your opinion, same as I am, son. Our disagreeing has nothing to do with you telling the truth the way you saw it. Justice depends on that, son."

Lucas McCain,
The Rifleman

❖

"I told 'em the truth and they fell for it."

Judge Harry Stone,
Night Court

❖

"I always believe in telling the truth—once you get caught."

Bill Parker,
Mr. Ed

❖

"Civilization has always depended on courtesy, rather than truth."

Zarkoff,
Blake's 7

❖

"The truer you are, the freer you get. It's automatic."

Kelly Robinson,
I Spy

❖

"A lie takes an awful lot of words, the truth takes very few."

Benevolent Love,
The Big Valley

❖

Mrs. Looney: "One way to confound your enemies is to tell them the truth. Did you ever notice how little attention people pay to the truth?"
Hoss Cartwright: "Yeah, now that you mention it."

Bonanza

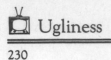
❖

"Sometimes the truth can be so unnecessary."

Remington Steele,
Remington Steele

Ugliness

Kingfish: "Madame Olga, I'm bringing my mother-in-law into your beauty parlor here this afternoon for a complete overhaul."
Madame Olga: "You make it sound like a big project."
Kingfish: "Well, Madame Olga, I'm gonna give you the problem with my mother-in-law. Have you ever been down to the beach and seen a grapefruit washed up on the sand? One that been in the water for three or four weeks and then washed up and left to dry in the sun for a few days?"
M. Olga: "Yes."
Kingfish: "Well, if you can get her lookin' that good, I'll be satisfied."

Amos 'n' Andy

❖

"You could throw her in the river and skim ugly for two days."

Granny,
The Beverly Hillbillies

The U.S.A.

"New Jersey announced today that they were adopting a new license-plate slogan: 'Try Our Creamy Thick Shakes.'"

David Letterman,
Late Night with David Letterman

❖

"California is the worst place in the world to be buried in. They get them earthquakes out there. They put you in your box in the ground there, and the earthquakes keep knocking you around. That way

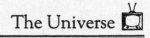
your bones don't get a chance to rest in peace they way they oughtta."

> **Archie Bunker,**
> *All in the Family*

❖

"It's a free country, except for the funeral expenses."

> **A cop,**
> *Mannix*

❖

"What's this I hear about about making Puerto Rico a steak? The next thing they'll be wanting is a salad, and then a baked potato."

> **Emily Litella (Gilda Radner),**
> *Saturday Night Live*

❖

"She's taking my son to Detroit—I mean, talk about child abuse. . . ."

> **Irate New Yorker [complaining about child custody fight],**
> *Barney Miller*

❖

"I moved to Minneapolis, where it was cold. . . . I figured I'd keep better."

> **Rhoda Morgenstern,**
> *Rhoda*

❖

"Land of my dreams—home of the Whopper."

> **Balki Bartokomous,**
> *Perfect Strangers*

The Universe

Caine: "Master Kan, what is it to be a man?"
Master Kan: "To be a man is to be one with the Universe."
Caine: "But what is the Universe?"
Master Kan: "Rather ask: what is *not* the Universe?"

> *Kung Fu*

Violence

"You can't solve every problem in the world with a good right hand."
Officer,
Baa Baa Black Sheep

❖

Victoria Barkley: "Violence never solved anything."
Nick Barkley: "Mother, there are times when you have to fight, no
matter what it leads to."
The Big Valley

❖

"Will shooting guns and making bombs make you men and not dogs?"
Caine,
Kung Fu

❖

"Those who live by the gun die by the neck."

Pappy Maverick,
Maverick

❖

"They do say, Mrs. M, that verbal insults hurt more than physical
pain. They are, of course, wrong as you will soon discover when I stick
this toasting fork in your head."
Edmund BlackAdder,
BlackAdder the Third

❖

Murphy: "He didn't try anything funny, did he?"
Mrs. Murphy: "Aside from trying to kill us, he was a perfect
gentleman."
Murphy's Law

❖

"You wanna hit me? Go ahead! Fine! Hit me! I'm not worried about
me. I'm not worried about you. It's these kids! If we can't teach our

children that fighting is not the answer, then we failed—as parents and as human beings. So, you can hit me, or you can shake my hand. The choice is yours."

Jason,
Growing Pains

❖

Agent 99: "Oh, Max, how terrible."
Maxwell Smart: "He deserved it, Ninety-nine. He was a KAOS killer."
Agent 99: "Sometimes I wonder if we're any better, Max."
Smart: "What are you talking about, Ninety-nine? We have to shoot and kill and destroy. We represent everything that's wholesome and good in the world."

Get Smart

War

"I will say one thing about the white man: when he gets hold of a good war, he don't let go of it."

Two Persons Baudine,
Quest

❖

"Louise, I can tell you a little bit about life, but I can't tell you anything about war. I don't think any woman can explain to another woman about war. It's an insanity that women just don't understand. It's . . . well, it's like falling down a hill. You can't stop and you can't change direction, and you're bound to get hurt."

Miss Kitty,
Gunsmoke

❖

Captain Kirk: "Well, there it is—war. We didn't want it, but we got it."
Spock: "Curious how often you humans manage to obtain that which you do not want."

Star Trek

❖

Maury Allen: "You spent two days and nights building this and now you've blown it to kingdom come? What the devil for?"
Hawkeye Pierce: "Senseless destruction is what war is all about."

M*A*S*H

❖

"Go to war. Keep the world safe for hypocrisy."

Laugh-In

❖

"Wars don't last forever. Only war does."

Hawkeye Pierce,
M*A*S*H

Weapons

"A weapon? No, only an instrument, neither good nor evil until men put it to use. And then, like so many of man's inventions, it can be used either to save lives or to destroy them, to make men sane or to drive them mad, to increase human understanding or to betray it. But it will be men who make the choice. By itself the instrument is nothing . . . until you add the human factor."

The Control Voice,
The Outer Limits

❖

"We have to have some sort of weapons besides our wits and good looks."

Nancy Drew,
The Nancy Drew Mystery Show

❖

"The tools of conquest do not necessarily come with bombs and explosions and fallout. There are weapons that are simply thoughts, attitudes, prejudices—to be found only in the minds of men."

Rod Serling,
The Twilight Zone

❖

"I think the bow and arrow has long been underrated as a weapon. Aesthetically, it is far superior to the revolver and can be just as effective without any unseemly powder burns. There is no danger of the victim suffering from lead poisoning, and it requires no silencer. In fact, if it is used properly, the entire weapon is a silencer. Of course, one must be careful. The bow and arrow can be very dangerous when in the wrong hands. Cupid, for example. . . ."

Alfred Hitchcock
Alfred Hitchcock Presents

Wine

"Beer is for the thirst. Wine . . . for the senses."

John Steed,
The Avengers

❖

"I like a wine that fights back."

John Steed,
The Avengers

❖

Six years and you haven't learned *anything*—it's *white* wine with Hershey Bars."

Harvey Barros,
Making the Grade

Winning

"There's nothing to winning, really. That is, if you happen to be blessed with a keen eye, an agile mind, and no scruples whatsoever."

Alfred Hitchcock,
Alfred Hitchcock Presents

❖

Jane Hathaway: "Chief, haven't you ever heard of the saying 'It's not whether you win or lose, it's how you play the game'?"
Mr. Drysdale: "Yes, I've heard it. And I consider it one of the most ridiculous statements ever made."

The Beverly Hillbillies

❖

Wilbur Post: "I'm counting on you to win tomorrow, but if you don't, be a good sport—lose with a smile."
Mr. Ed: "I'd rather win with a sneer!"

Mr. Ed

❖

"It's just amazing to me that you're not a better loser, Cliff. After all, you have had a lot of practice."

J.R. Ewing,
Dallas

❖

"As my Great Aunt Maude always said, 'If you can't win the game, the next best thing is to upset the chessboard.' "

Artemis Gordon,
The Wild, Wild West

❖

"The only time you quit when you're winning is after you've won it all."

Pappy Maverick,
Maverick

A Woman's Place

Julie McCoy: "Today's woman doesn't wait for the phone to ring. She places the call herself."

Passenger: "Really?"
Julie: "Yes, she refuses to float down the stream of life. She paddles her own canoe—and so can you."

The Love Boat

❖

"A woman's place is in the car."

Vinnie Barbarino,
Welcome Back, Kotter

❖

Althea: "Miss Kitty, have you ever been in love?"
Miss Kitty: "I guess every girl falls in love once."
Althea: "But you didn't want to get married?"
Miss Kitty: "No."
Althea: "Why not?"
Miss Kitty: "I guess I wasn't asked by the right man."
Althea: "You could ask him."
Miss Kitty: "Well, Althea, it's a sad state of affairs, but girls just aren't supposed to do that."

Gunsmoke

❖

"It's a man's work to make a mess and a woman's work to clean it up afterwards."

Luke Macahan,
How the West Was Won

❖

"You should be a very happy woman. You're beautiful, you got a nice home, three great kids, a husband who adores you. That oughta be enough for any gal."

Danny Williams [to his wife],
Make Room for Daddy

❖

David Addison: "What about the rights women have dropped their mops for? Scratched and clawed for? Broken nails for? You think just because your voice is higher, your chest is bumpier, that you are entitled to roadside service everytime your car blows a tire in the rain? Doesn't it seem a little passé to you that a woman should expect a man's help every time there's trouble?"

Moonlighting

❖

"The women of our family have always stood behind our men. We've always been ready to put our head on the block and our shoulder to the tombstones."

Lily Munster,
The Munsters

❖

"You know something? There's times when a woman can be too smart for her own good—even if she *is* a good cook."

Marshal Matt Dillon,
Gunsmoke

❖

Gracie Allen: "You can't give up, Blanche. Women don't do that. Look at Betsy Ross, Martha Washington—they didn't give up. Look at Nina Jones."
Blanche Morton: "Nina Jones?"
Gracie: "I never heard of her either, because she gave up."

The George Burns and Gracie Allen Show

A Woman's Work

"Washing dishes, making beds, and cooking beans hardly qualifies a person as a building contractor."

Jim Anderson,
Father Knows Best

❖

Ralph Kramden: "No wife of mine is gonna work. I got my pride. You know, no Kramden woman has ever supported her husband. The Kramden men are the workers in the family."

Alice Kramden: "Wait a minute, Ralph. What about your father? For a long time there he didn't work at all."

Ralph: "But neither did my mother. At least he kept his pride, Alice —he went on relief!"

The Honeymooners

❖

Larry Appleton: "Balki, don't you know what that woman does for a living? Let's just say that she's in the world's oldest profession."

Balki Bartokomous: "Oh! She's a sheepherder."

Perfect Strangers

❖

Harry Von Zell: "Gracie, why are you washing clean dishes?"

Gracie Allen: "I haven't any dirty ones. I've been too upset to eat."

Harry: "You *are* upset."

Gracie: "Yes, but upset or not, a woman has to do her housework."

The George Burns and Gracie Allen Show

❖

"Perhaps crimefighting is better left to the men, Batgirl, perhaps not. But this isn't exactly women's work."

Batman

❖

[Ozzie Nelson has been spending a lot of his time as a volunteer fireman.]

Harriet Nelson: "You know, if they let women in the fire department, then I'd see more of you."

Ozzie Nelson: "Are you kidding? You gals take too long to dress."

Harriet: "Oh, I don't know—we can be pretty quick."

Ozzie: "By the time you got your makeup on, the fire'd be out."

The Adventures of Ozzie and Harriet

❖

Lawyer [after Cagney submits to a drug test]: "You threw your constitutional rights out the window! Remember the Fifth Amendment?"

Chris Cagney: "David, it's just part of the job. Some days you pound the streets, some days you pee in bottles."

Cagney & Lacey

❖

Laura Petrie: "Honey, won't you just let me try to help you?"

Rob Petrie: "Honey, I just don't think you and I would be happy as marriage partners *and* business partners."

Laura: "Isn't that silly, darling. Don't you realize that in the office *you'd* be the boss! You know what I mean, darling. It's just that I want to do something to help you."

Rob: "If you want to do something to help me, then feed me."

The Dick Van Dyke Show

❖

[To housekeeper] "Now look, you've got a million things to do for the Women's Rights party tonight—you can fix the hors d'oeuvres, vacuum the living room, dust the furniture, bake the cookies."

Maude Findlay,
Maude

Women

Dwayne Schneider: "A woman is like a bathtub full of water—once you get it hot, it doesn't cool off too fast."

Barbara Cooper: "And once it does, it has a ring."

One Day at a Time

❖

"There's no getting around it. Women cost money."

Bud Anderson,
Father Know's Best

❖

Cinnamon Carter: "Anything that is exciting is dangerous."
Politician: "I'm told that women can be dangerous."
Cinnamon: "That depends on the woman."

Mission: Impossible

❖

Maddie Hayes: "You men, always wanting to put us up on a pedestal
or down in the gutter."
David Addison: "That way we can either look up your skirts or down
your blouses."

Moonlighting

❖

"You know women—they hear goodbye in your voice and their lower
lip starts trembling. The next thing you know you're buying them
something fuel-injected."

Charles Kincaid,
Double Trouble

❖

"A woman is like an appendix . . . she's something a man is better off
without."

Popeye,
The Popeye Cartoon Show

❖

"Women always have to have a reason for everything."

Politician,
Mission: Impossible

❖

"A dame is like a bottle of milk . . . if she hangs around long enough
she turns sour."

Bluto,
Popeye

"It's not the frivolity of women that makes them so intolerable. It's their ghastly enthusiasm."

Horace Rumpole,
Rumpole of the Bailey

❖

"Women: You can't live with them, can't leave 'em on the curb when you're done with them."

David Addison,
Moonlighting

❖

"Women: Can't live with 'em, can't stuff 'em in a sack."

Larry,
Newhart

Women: The Enigma

"It's been proven through history that wimmin's a mystery."

Popeye,
The Popeye Cartoon Show

❖

"Nothing gets a man more than a woman he can't understand."

Millie Foster,
Mayberry, R.F.D.

❖

Johnny Fever: "I don't know, Les, what do women want?"
Les Nessman: "Tupperware?"

WKRP in Cincinnati

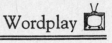
❖

"I never met a man yet that didn't know all there was about women."
Miss Kitty,
Gunsmoke

❖

"I'll never understand women if I live to be thirty!"
Richard Harrison,
The Patty Duke Show

Wordplay

"Claustrophobia? It's a dreadful fear of Santa Claus."
Vinnie Barbarino,
Welcome Back, Kotter

❖

Doctor Who: "I don't care much for the word 'impregnable.' Sounds a bit too much like 'unsinkable.'"
Harry: "What's wrong with 'unsinkable?' "
Doctor Who: "Nothing. As the iceberg said to the Titanic: 'glug, glug, glug.' "
Doctor Who

❖

Elliott Carlin: "I think I'm overcoming my agoraphobia."
Bob Hartley: "I didn't know you had a fear of open places."
Carlin: "I thought it was a fear of agricultural products. Anyway, wheat doesn't scare me anymore."
The Bob Newhart Show

❖

"Miss Olam, you should never assume, because when you assume, you make an *ass* of *u* and *me*."
Felix Unger,
The Odd Couple

❖

"You ever notice the long words Harry uses? An ordinary man could take one of Harry's words, break it into pieces, and have enough for a whole day's conversation."

George Burns,
The George Burns and Gracie Allen Show

❖

"You said, 'but.' I've put my finger on the whole trouble. You're a 'but' man. Don't say 'but.' That little word 'but' is the difference between success and failure. Henry Ford said 'I'm going to invent the automobile,' and Arthur T. Flanken said 'But—.' Now we watch Fords go by. Did you ever watch an Arthur T. Flanken go by? Did you?"

Sgt. Ernie Bilko,
The Phil Silvers Show

❖

"Someone did a study of the three most-often-heard phrases in New York City. One is, 'Hey, taxi.' Two is, 'What train do I take to get to Bloomingdale's?' And three is, 'Don't worry. It's just a flesh wound.' "

David Letterman,
Late Night with David Letterman

❖

Neighbor: "George, your office has that certain *je ne sais quoi.* . . ."
George Jefferson: "Not anymore—I just had it exterminated yesterday."

The Jeffersons

❖

Henry: "We love the ambience of Mel's Diner."
Customer: "What's ambience?"
Vera: "That's what they pick you up in after you've eaten Mel's food."

Alice

❖

"A little cheese for the three of us—a little fromage a trois."

Mork,
Mork and Mindy

❖

"Avant-garde. . . . That's French for 'off-Broadway garbage.' "

Buddy Sorrell,
The Dick Van Dyke Show

Work

"My old Pappy used to say, 'Son, hard work never hurt anyone—who didn't do it.' "

Bart Maverick,
Maverick

❖

"My Great Aunt Maude used to say that enthusiasm is a sure sign a man loves his work."

Artemus Gordon,
The Wild, Wild West

❖

Mindy McConnell: "Mork, I'll be happy to show you around after work."
Mork: "Work?"
Mindy: "Oh yes, most people have to work for a living."
Mork: "Hm-m-m. What a novel concept."

Mork and Mindy

❖

The Skipper: "Hard work never hurt anybody."
Thurston Howell III: "Well, it never helped anyone either."

Gilligan's Island

"I don't have anything against work. I just figure, why deprive somebody who really loves it?"

Dobie Gillis,
The Many Loves of Dobie Gillis

❖

Napoleon Solo: "Are you free?"
Illya Kuryakin: "No man is free who has to work for a living. But I am available."

The Man from U.N.C.L.E.

❖

Burt Campbell: "I'm building a future so you can have everything you ever wanted. . . . I need to do it for me, to prove I can do it."
Mary Campbell: "Tomorrow when you're driving home and some drunk jumps over the center divider and you wind up dead, you will have spent the last days and nights of your life working."

Soap

❖

"When you have a job that you love . . . you have to do it yourself."

The Good Fairy,
Bewitched

❖

"When you dig a hole in the earth, you owe it to the earth to fill it back up with something better. That's called work."

Marshal Matt Dillon,
Gunsmoke

❖

"When a man loses his appetite for honest work, he already has one foot in the grave."

Little John,
The Adventures of Robin Hood

❖

"Early to bed and early to rise is the curse of the working class."

Pappy Maverick,
Maverick

❖

[Jethro gets a job delivering newspapers.]
Granny: "Ain't he just a paperboy?"
Jed Clampett: "Oh no, Granny. He's watcha call 'Deputy District Circulation Chief in Charge o' Home Distribution.' Well, Jethro, yore a workin' man now. Make us proud a ya."
Granny: "Always remember, 'A job worth doin' is worth two in the bush!' "

The Beverly Hillbillies

❖

"Remember, the reward of a job well done is to do it."

Gil Halswell,
Trackdown

❖

"Don't impose too long on a man's hospitality; he's liable to put you to work."

Pappy Maverick,
Maverick

Work: Promotions

"The meek may inherit the earth, but it's the grumpy who get promoted."

Father Francis Mulcahy,
*M*A*S*H*

❖

"The way I figure it, leaving a job you really love for one that pays more money isn't necessarily a promotion."

Gabe Kotter,
Welcome Back, Kotter

Work: View from the Top

"Nobody has ever stood up to me the way you did, Rush. I find you bold, forceful, a man of conviction—three qualities I *despise* in an employee."

Mr. Wainwright III,
Too Close for Comfort

❖

Maxwell Smart: "Sometimes I wonder if we're just not attracting the right kind of dedicated men."
The Chief: "I know, Max. All they're interested in is wine, women, and song."
Smart: "That's not exactly true, Chief. I've never heard the men singing."

Get Smart

❖

Mel Cooley: "You can't be replaced."
Buddy Sorrell: "Why?"
Mel: "Because I don't know what you are!"

The Dick Van Dyke Show

❖

"You would make a fine manager. You're sneakier than I thought."

Congressman Morley,
The Farmer's Daughter

"We don't care. We don't have to. We're the phone company."

Lily Tomlin,
Laugh-In

Work: You're Fired

Rob Petrie: "He won't fire me. It'll look bad in the papers."
Buddy Sorrell: "Yeah. . . . It looks bad to fire a guy the same day you kill him."

The Dick Van Dyke Show

❖

"I'm very bad at firing people, Mr. Grant. I once had to move rather than fire a housekeeper."

Mary Richards,
The Mary Tyler Moore Show

❖

Samantha Stevens: "Darrin may lose his job!"
Aunt Clara [to Darrin]: "Oh, I think that's splendid. That way you can spend more time at home. Oh, I'm happy for you. I just knew it was going to be a lucky weekend for both of you."

Bewitched

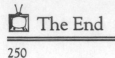
The End

"Now it's time to say goodbye to all our company. . . ."

The Mouseketeers
The Mickey Mouse Club

❖

"It's over. It's done. It's yesterday's mashed potatoes."

Larry Appleton,
Perfect Strangers

❖

"Adios. . . . That's goodbye in Spanish. Also, carbolic acid. That's goodbye in any language."

Roger Hanover,
The Andy Griffith Show

❖

"Until we meet again, may the good Lord take a liking to you."

Roy Rogers,
The Roy Rogers Show

❖

"May the good fairy sprinkle stardust on your bippy."
Dick Martin,
Laugh-In

❖

"Aloha, Suckers!"
Jack Lord,
Hawaii Five-0

Acknowledgments

Many hundreds of viewing hours were spent gathering material for this book. Fortunately, we didn't have to do all the viewing ourselves. An enthusiastic group of TV fans assisted us with research, gathering quotes from their favorite programs and diligently supplying them to us over a twelve-month period. Many watched taped programs over and over, trying to get every word of every quote exactly right; others got in the habit of regularly watching TV with a pad and pencil in hand.

We are deeply indebted to these folks; it's as much their book as it is ours, and so we hope they're pleased with the result of their collective labors. Thanks a million to:

Linda Adams
Diane Albert
Debra Anderson
Peter Angelopolous
Jim Aschbacher
Shirley Backus
Lori Beatty
Cheryl Blythe
Kevin Bohn
Christina Bonner
Terry Bowers
Warren Breed
Jon Burlingame
Big Bucks Burnett
Zak Burns
Bruce Button
Chris Campbell
Ed Carter
Richard Chen
Charles Cino
Bruce Clark (The Prisoner
    Appreciation Society)
Jim Clark (The Andy Griffith
    Rerun Watchers Club)
John Carman
Elizabeth Cleary
Tom Coates
Morjana Lee Coffman (The Star
    Trek Welcomittee)

Max Allan Collins
Patsy Cothran
Steve Cox
Kim Crow
Jim Davidson (The National
    Association for the
    Advancement of Perry Mason)
Ginny Daye
Jeannine Deubel
Lonna Doyle
Petera Doziotti
Randall Dunford
Jeff Edwards
Lee Falcon
William Felchner
Linda Kay Fenner
Lois Ferrai
Iris Flinker
Susan Flinker
Brenda Fraunfelter
Sue Gessford
Anthony Gliozzo
Fred Grandinetti
Gary Grossman
Dan Gunning
Ross Halper
Beth Hathaway
Jerri Hathaway
Jon Heitland

Gary Hobisch
Vicki Holt
Dave Huson
Mary Ann Johanson
Sharon Joy (Spotlight Starman)
Ken Kaffke
Alice Kahn
David Keil
Tom Kelly
Mark Kirby
T.C. Kirkham
Kay Kirkland
Tom Kleinschmidt
Sandra Konte
K.N. Kricker
Nancy Long
Lynn Lorton
Mark Lungo
Kathleen McCullough
Donna McCrohan
Lynda Mendoza
Julian Metzger
Flint Mitchell
Rick Mitz
Beth Muramoto
Koko Nakao
Jim Nolt
Glenda O'Keefe
Don Overly, Jr.
Bill Parisho

John Peel
Steven Peel
Lee Poleske
L. Jeanne Powers
Alan Press
Dawn Rice
Pat Rodda
Brenda Royce
Susan Sackett
Lynda Sappington
David Schow
Ann Scrivener
Michael Shore
Capt. and Mrs. Howard A. Sine
Jeff Sorenson
Glen Stripling
Barb Sweigart
Kayleen Sybrandt
Ann C. Teipen
Richard Tharp
Ted Tucker
Walter von Bosau
Robert Waldsdorff
Doree Ward
Jill S. Wells
Hoppy Weschler
Teddi Williams
Ronnie Wise
R. Allan Young
Marc Scott Zicree

Special thanks, also, to our editor, Melissa Schwarz, and to Andy
Sohn, Rachel Blau, and Lauren Cherry for design and production of
this book. Rachel Blau, Katherine Dittrich, and Moira Hughes proof-
read. Lonnie Graham, eminent pop psychologist, created the TV
icon. Herb Caen, John Carman, Mike Duffy, Jim Slotek, Jeff Edwards,
and others got the word out. The final boards were printed at Fifth
Street Computer Services, Jay Nitschke's new Berkeley establishment.

Index

The Abbott and Costello Show, 172
The Addams Family, 14, 25, 42, 59, 78, 81, 91,
 94, 96, 99, 108, 114, 118, 122, 132, 147, 160,
 168, 184, 191, 195, 200, 215, 224
The Adventures of Felix the Cat, 100, 118
The Adventures of Ozzie and Harriet, 239
The Adventures of Robin Hood, 43, 247
The Adventures of Sir Lancelot, 212
The Adventures of Superman, 211
ALF, 26, 194
Alfred Hitchcock Presents, 14, 54, 108, 113,
 131, 133, 140, 149, 152, 156, 175, 185, 210,
 217, 223, 225, 235
Alice, 31, 105, 134, 212, 244
All in the Family, 11, 23, 46, 47, 55, 64, 83, 84,
 93, 139, 155, 206, 209, 222, 227, 231
Amos 'n' Andy, 9, 29, 110, 117, 136, 150, 190,
 206, 230,
The Andy Griffith Show, 15, 27, 34, 60, 62, 66,
 75, 81, 91, 98, 107, 120, 128, 152, 181, 198,
 199, 217, 223, 250
Annie McGuire, 69, 184
Another World, 26
Art Linkletter's House Party, 17, 28, 34, 79,
 169, 173, 192
Atom Ant, 89
The Avengers, 178, 235
Baa Baa Black Sheep, 232
Banacek, 39
Barnaby Jones, 40, 78, 111
Barney Miller, 14, 30, 34, 36, 48, 65, 70, 80,
 87, 106, 154, 159, 160, 190, 224, 231
Batman, 58, 65, 66, 89, 90, 108, 116, 126, 141,
 154, 177, 178, 239
Battlestar Galactica, 59
Beauty and the Beast, 127
The Beverly Hillbillies, 18, 29, 61, 84, 86, 100,
 103, 132, 185, 190, 215, 230, 236, 247
Bewitched, 17, 38, 50, 69, 72, 80, 89, 138, 143,
 147, 196, 246, 249
The Big Valley, 70, 121, 156, 166, 194, 229,
 232
BlackAdder II, 190
BlackAdder the Third, 232
Blake's 7, 24, 63, 67, 104, 116, 186, 190, 213,
 227, 229
The Bob Newhart Show, 39, 103, 145, 146,
 154, 182, 185, 226, 229
Bonanza, 29, 69, 73, 81, 83, 91, 127, 182, 185,
 226, 229
Bosom Buddies, 31, 119, 214
Bozo's Circus, 180
Bret Maverick, 29
The Bugs Bunny Show, 26, 86, 156, 198, 226
The Bullwinkle Show, 36, 78, 96, 98, 113, 153,
 169, 197, 210, 220

Burke's Law, 46
Cagney & Lacey, 13, 18, 38, 38, 41, 105, 167,
 173, 203, 240
Candid Camera, 69, 79, 148, 168, 202
Captain Penny, 147
Car 54, Where Are You?, 33, 145, 222
CBS News, 220
Cheers, 12, 18, 19, 54, 58, 103, 104, 115, 118,
 121, 126, 190, 192, 197, 201, 225, 228
Chico and the Man, 63, 64, 137, 164, 205
The City of Angels, 103, 127, 205
Combat, 43
Commercials, 42, 88, 164, 142
The Cosby Show, 73, 97, 136, 166, 215
Crime Story, 121
Crossroads, 196
Daktari, 151
Dallas, 88, 92, 149, 157, 173, 189, 204, 236
Daniel Boone, 68, 158
Dark Shadows, 52
The Days and Nights of Molly Dodd, 101
Dear John, 134
Designing Women, 83, 158, 170
The Devlin Connection, 39
The Dick Cavett Show, 200
The Dick Van Dyke Show, 14, 18, 21, 44, 48,
 52, 129, 133, 166, 240, 245, 248, 249
Doctor Who, 67, 87, 90, 99, 120, 143, 167,
 194, 211, 243
The Donna Reed Show, 179
Double Trouble, 43, 113, 132, 133, 159, 241
Dragnet, 23, 35, 36, 47, 138
Dynasty, 145
The Ed Wynn Show, 222,
Eisenhower and Lutz, 17
Empty Nest, 50, 56
The Ernie Kovacs Show, 221
Falcon Crest, 80
Family, 15
Family Ties, 88, 153, 163, 165, 203, 204
Fantasy Island, 15, 57
The Farmer's Daughter, 248
Father Knows Best, 71, 93, 110, 111, 115,
 179, 183, 192, 213, 226, 238, 240
Filthy Rich, 200
A Fine Romance, 138
The Flintstones, 142, 225
The Flying Nun, 114, 128
The Fugitive, 115, 119
The Gale Storm Show, 212
The George Burns and Gracie Allen Show,
 20, 32, 76, 94, 101, 131, 138, 139, 157, 182,
 185, 198, 206, 210, 222, 238, 239, 244
Get Smart, 65, 123, 124, 125, 135, 154, 163,
 174, 192, 233, 248

The Ghost and Mrs. Muir, 136
Gilligan's Island, 22, 24, 27, 43, 120, 150, 177, 224, 245
The Golden Girls, 9, 12, 16, 40, 50, 51, 56, 85, 113, 119, 133, 148, 154, 174, 184, 194, 200
Gomer Pyle, 110
Good Times, 30, 41
The Greatest American Hero, 95, 105
Green Acres, 43, 80
Growing Pains, 101, 124, 140, 233
Gumby, 208
Gunsmoke, 30, 34, 63, 72, 108, 150, 226, 233, 237, 238, 243, 246
Haig, Alexander, 113
Happy Days, 33, 60, 98, 102, 111, 114, 123, 163, 202
Hardcastle and McCormick, 95
The Hardy Boys, 205
Hart to Hart, 32
Have Gun, Will Travel, 42, 121
Hawaii Five-O, 87, 101, 224, 250
Head of the Class, 42
Here Come the Brides, 38
Hill Street Blues, 36, 45, 64, 109, 148, 155, 179, 194
The Hit Squad, 225
The Hitchhiker's Guide to the Galaxy, 39, 40, 78, 114, 118, 133, 197
Hogan's Heroes, 176
The Hollywood Palace, 215
Hollywood Squares, 72
The Honeymooners, 52, 72, 110, 124, 134, 139, 150, 151, 171, 172, 181, 195, 196, 218, 239
Hot Metal, 37, 67, 68
House Calls, 171
How the West Was Won, 237
The Howdy Doody Show, 11, 12, 158
I Dream of Jeannie, 19, 186
I Love Lucy, 21, 29, 38, 140, 141, 143, 176, 226
I Married Dora, 88
I Married Joan, 141
I Spy, 116, 125, 178, 228, 229
The Incredible Hulk, 105, 157
Iron Horse, 75
The Jeffersons, 11, 60, 72, 176, 213, 244
Jeopardy, 119
Jonny Quest, 12
The Judy Garland Show, 221
Julia, 63
Kate and Allie, 146
Kaz, 109, 207
Kung Fu, 39, 67, 74, 79, 92, 106, 107, 111, 124, 155, 162, 167, 168, 195, 199, 205, 212, 231, 232
L.A. Law, 186
Late Night with David Letterman, 13, 55, 106, 159, 160, 174, 230, 244

Laugh-In, 25, 55, 56, 155, 198, 209, 215, 234, 249, 250
Laverne and Shirley, 25, 49, 57, 104
Leave It to Beaver, 9, 24, 27, 46, 67, 71, 73, 90, 96, 98, 99, 112, 115, 142, 148, 166, 174, 183, 185, 189, 193, 195, 215
The Life and Legend of Wyatt Earp, 120
The Lone Ranger, 68
Lost in Space, 13, 42, 45, 58, 63, 67, 68, 129, 196, 207
Lou Grant, 228
Love Boat, 169, 237
Love That Bob, 49
M*A*S*H, 10, 16, 23, 42, 56, 71, 75, 79, 105, 109, 116, 125, 141, 151, 156, 161, 171, 187, 219, 224, 234, 247
MacGyver, 41, 67
Magnum, P.I., 43, 126, 131, 143, 154, 170, 179, 194
Make Room for Daddy, 16, 22, 228, 237
Making the Grade, 235
Mama's Family, 70, 117
The Man from Atlantis, 178
The Man from U.N.C.L.E., 49, 51, 66, 74, 121, 149, 172, 193, 246
Mannix, 231
The Many Loves of Dobie Gillis, 22, 27, 28, 56, 73, 97, 107, 110, 123, 165, 166, 176, 246
Married...with Children, 134, 144, 187
Mary Hartman, Mary Hartman, 10, 20, 26, 44, 61, 84, 85, 91, 158, 223
The Mary Tyler Moore Show, 11, 17, 21, 53, 61, 66, 76, 128, 153, 160, 170, 171, 175, 180, 187, 201, 221, 222, 249
Maude, 10, 20, 101, 240
Maverick, 24, 45, 52, 62, 71, 75, 77, 80, 83, 85, 92, 99, 108, 129, 135, 149, 167, 180, 188, 199, 211, 212, 213, 232, 236, 245, 246
Max Headroom, 23, 58, 68, 130, 208, 220
Mayberry, R.F.D., 242
McMillan and Wife, 31
Miami Vice, 39, 43, 104, 207
The Mickey Mouse Club, 82, 88, 112, 188, 250
Midnight Caller, 11
Mission: Impossible, 177, 241
Mr. Ed, 11, 13, 20, 94, 102, 124, 136, 152, 158, 163, 186, 209, 214, 229, 236
The Monkees, 116, 130, 221
Monty Python's Flying Circus, 40, 178
Moonlighting, 9, 52, 57, 103, 122, 175, 177, 204, 208, 238, 241, 242
Mork and Mindy, 37, 90, 102, 120, 145, 149, 152, 169, 173, 179, 183, 192, 204, 245
The Munsters, 14, 33, 53, 57, 91, 96, 130, 132, 153, 161, 164, 171, 191, 192, 206, 219, 221, 227, 238
Murder, She Wrote, 109
Murphy's Law, 232
My Favorite Martian, 48, 59, 81, 104, 114, 116, 147, 223

My Mother the Car, 222
My Three Sons, 19, 119, 139
NBC News, 54
Naked City, 34, 113
The Nancy Drew Mystery Show, 23
Nero Wolfe, 109
The New Adventures of Mighty Mouse, 38, 127, 129, 219, 220
Newhart, 16, 41, 58, 61, 84, 85, 86, 87, 95, 100, 117, 128, 137, 151, 187, 219, 220, 242
The Newlywed Game, 77
Night Court, 45, 51, 145, 155, 229
Noble House, 122
The Odd Couple, 16, 50, 61, 72, 75, 76, 77, 82, 94, 111, 161, 191, 193, 208, 209, 243
O'Hara, 122
One Day at a Time, 33, 55, 130, 137, 144, 164, 169, 200, 240
The Oregon Trail, 170
The Original Talking Max Headroom Show, 10
Our Miss Brooks, 46, 136
The Outer Limits, 10, 15, 38, 41, 46, 58, 59, 65, 74, 121, 128, 130, 146, 157, 172, 228, 234
The Paper Chase, 86
The Patty Duke Show, 24, 48, 243
Pee-Wee's Playhouse, 98, 184
Perfect Strangers, 62, 94, 99, 100, 112, 196, 205, 214, 231, 239, 250
Perry Mason, 53, 112, 114, 136, 165, 227, 228
Peter Gunn, 36
The Phil Silvers Show, 17, 50, 82, 134, 151, 164, 176, 244
The Planet of the Apes, 156
Police Squad!, 123, 202, 209, 212
The Popeye Cartoon Show, 81, 89, 102, 162, 174, 216, 241, 242
The Powers of Matthew Star, 78
The Prisoner, 103, 105, 122, 124, 151, 169, 173, 183, 205
Queen for a Day, 115
Quest, 232
Quincy, 66, 94
The Real McCoys, 77, 219
Remington Steele, 14, 30, 43, 92, 152, 170, 183, 186, 187, 211, 230
Rhoda, 75, 159, 231
The Rifleman, 94, 229
Riptide, 21, 32, 131, 142, 144
The Rockford Files, 53, 77, 80, 82, 92, 146, 148, 170, 172, 175, 181
Roseanne, 20, 22, 44, 140, 147, 148, 207
Rosetti and Ryan, 9
Route 66, 181
The Roy Rogers Show, 110, 250
Rumpole of the Bailey, 93, 109, 242
Ryan's Hope, 19
SCTV, 18, 29, 51, 71, 95

The Saint, 35, 55, 120, 199
Sanford and Son, 9, 64, 87, 176, 184, 189
Saturday Night Live, 31, 195, 221, 231
Sesame Street, 12
77 Sunset Strip, 24, 31
Sidekicks, 64
Simon and Simon, 26, 40, 41, 89, 125, 150, 193, 204, 226
Soap, 53, 64, 70, 133, 147, 188, 199, 200, 202, 246
Sonny Spoon, 125
The Soupy Sales Show, 216
The Slap Maxwell Story, 78, 88, 187, 203, 209
Space: 1999, 55, 59, 83, 84, 105, 213
Star Trek, 65, 69, 104, 122, 124, 125, 143, 155, 157, 158, 162, 173, 201, 232
Star Trek: The Next Generation, 211
Starman, 27, 73, 123, 156, 168, 186, 191, 227
Starsky and Hutch, 30, 118, 132, 180, 227
Stingray, 119, 167, 168, 177, 207
The Streets of San Francsico, 49, 108
Supermarket Sweep, 203
The Tall Man, 44
Tattinger's, 19, 205
Taxi, 10, 19, 25, 31, 40, 76, 81, 93, 97, 100, 112, 118, 123, 135, 143, 144, 145, 146, 149, 182, 188, 208, 213, 223
Tenspeed and Brown Shoe, 45
Thirtysomething, 166
Three's Company, 50, 141, 161
Thriller, 13, 196
The Time Tunnel, 82
Together We Stand, 128
Too Close for Comfort, 48, 248
Trackdown, 12, 44, 45, 246
Trapper John, M.D., 199
The Trouble with Father, 218
The Twilight Zone, 22, 28, 38, 47, 48, 52, 57, 74, 87, 129, 131, 214, 234
Underdog, 171
The Untouchables, 37, 47
Valerie, 41
Van Dyke, 51
Voyage to the Bottom of the Sea, 59, 163, 195
Welcome Back, Kotter, 28, 68, 84, 91, 97, 130, 139, 180, 201, 237, 243, 248
The Widow Cody, 46
The Wild, Wild West, 40, 70, 191, 194, 208, 236, 245
Wiseguy, 119
WKRP in Cincinnati, 23, 93, 144, 165, 178, 225, 242
The Wonder Years, 51, 74, 90, 97, 201
You Bet Your Life, 18, 54, 62, 71, 85, 127, 138, 191, 206
Young Maverick, 174
The Young Rebels, 168
Your Show of Shows, 25, 54, 57, 61, 95, 138, 181, 207, 216

Calling All TV Fans:

We're already straining our eyeballs gathering material for the second volume of *Primetime Proverbs*. Since you're glued to the tube anyway, why not give us a hand?

Contact us at:
1400 Shattuck Ave.
Suite 25
Berkeley, CA 94709